THIS IS MY STORY

BUT IT IS NOT MY LIFE

THIS IS MY STORY

BUT IT IS NOT MY LIFE

STORIES FROM WOMEN WHO CLIMBED BACK

LA DETRA WHITE

Cathy, thank you so much for being a sister!

La Detra 3.2016

For a seed to achieve it's greatest expression,
it must come completely undone.
The shell cracks, it's insides come
out and everything changes.
To someone who doesn't understand growth,
it would look like complete destruction.

Cynthia Occelli

Praise for

This is my story, but this is not my life

When La Detra posted a picture of this book's cover, I felt an immediate unction to pray for this project and everyone involved in sharing their story. Prayer is a powerful tool that God gives us that encourages our own soul while simultaneously empowering others.

One of the weapons we have in overcoming the enemy or any circumstance is sharing our testimony. Revelations 12:11 declares "And they overcame by the blood of the Lamb and the word of their testimony." Sharing our stories of God's faithfulness and power in our lives activates His overcoming power in our lives and in the lives of others. As we testify, our words bring life and become conduits of grace to others. Likewise as Marianne Williamson stated, "As we let our own light shine, we unconsciously give other people permission to do the same. As we are liberated from our own fear, our presence automatically liberates others."

"Lord Jesus, I thank You now for the deliverance that You have brought and continue to bring in the lives of all who are sharing their stories in this book. Thank You also for the deliverance and power that is coming to every person who reads this book. Thank You that Your kingdom is advancing and overcoming every dark place to all who encounter, touch, edit, print, promote, invest in this project. No weapon formed against it will prosper and is cast down now in the name of Jesus. May You, Lord Jesus, continue to cover and bless La Detra, as she stewards this divinely inspired project into fruition. Multiply the grace in her life to advance your kingdom Lord Jesus in the marketplace. Bless her family and the works of her hands in Jesus name! Amen

SHARON BRYANT ZIMMERMAN, FRIEND.

Acknowledgements

First, giving all honor to God who made me unbelievably flawed and perfectly awesome. To Him, I give my praise. I thank the universe for tolerating my stubborn insertion to be free and to be heard. It can't always be easy to feel my nudging. I hope I have given much more than I have taken.

I thank my family, especially my husband Bob, who has never once stood in the way of my putting a great idea into action. I love you more than I can ever tell you in words. I hope I have shown you in every way I can muster. I thank my children, especially during those times when I have put your lives on hold to reach milestones related to this book. You have been the best children a Momma could ask for.

I thank the contributors to this book, each of you. We have begun a wondrous work. I could not have done any of it without your "I'm in."

I thank my editors: Nancy Eder, Pia Forbes, and Teresa B. Pernini. Y'all put the sauce on this. I appreciate you so very much. I learned so much from you along the way.

I thank Marta from Poland for the beautiful cover design. I long to meet you and hug your beautiful neck.

I offer special thanks to Curtis Bunn, who kept asking, "What are you waiting for?" long after I had run out of excuses. You are a friend above friends.

Readers, here we go. Grab a hot cup of something and let's do this right!

Love to all,

LW

TABLE OF CONTENTS

BETRAYAL

I was...
A broken vessel
A child, sexually molested by a family member
A child, wanting to be loved in the right way

I am...
A work in progress
Fearfully and wonderfully made
A mouthpiece for the voiceless

"When you write the story of your life, don't let anyone else hold the pen..."
~WRITER UNKNOWN

It took me years to understand the meaning of the aforementioned quote. This message imparts what I've been challenged to do: hold my own pen and write the story of my life! My story may shock some, but it may elevate and release others from despair; from hopelessness; from fear. It is my prayer that the words I share in this small passage will reach at least one woman or man, sink into their being and bring forth a new creature—one who is not ashamed of who he or she is, but rather, blessed beyond imagination, for speaking the truth!

Years of experiencing child sexual molestation; a mother who, in my child mind, I believed, didn't love me enough to comfort and protect me from my molester; years of broken promises from the men I loved; years of disappointment in others who took advantage of me; years of self-hatred, self-denial, and the lying, stealing, manipulating, sexual promiscuity that resulted from my trauma have made me a stronger, more viable person who is not afraid to speak out and tell the truth about my life so that others can experience the overwhelming blessing of release.

When I was a girl of maybe 6 years old, my mother started dating the man who would become her third husband and, later, her widower. One of my two childhood memories of this man is that he would come to our apartment in the Ida B. Wells Public Housing Project while she was at work to check on me and my two brothers. The other memory is of him taking my innocence from me, forcing his penis into my mouth.

He told me to not utter a word to my mother, and for years, I never did. But my brother did. He told my mother that her husband was a child molester. And afterward, my life became a living hell for years.

Wow. There it is in black and white. I was forced to perform oral sex on a man with whom I would share a home until I moved into my own place with my children.

As a child, I thought, This can't be right! Isn't this what grown men and women, husbands and wives, do? How long will he keep doing this? God, I'm a child—right?

So many questions ran through my child's brain, but I got no answers, because I never uttered them out loud.

The molestation continued. Two to three times a week, he'd send my brothers to the store and make me play with his penis, stroking it while sitting on his lap. I was afraid, but not afraid enough to tell my momma, because I was afraid of what she might do to me!

One weekend, my mother went out of town to visit her friend in Kentucky and left me there with him. My bedroom was in the back of our large apartment. One night, while my two brothers slept, he tipped into my room like a thief in the night. I pretended to be asleep until he began pulling at my panties. Once he took my panties off, I remember him climbing on top of me and attempting to put his penis in my vagina. I let out a loud scream because of the pain. He had the nerve to tell me to be quiet and tried again to rape me, but I kept trying to scream. After the third attempt, he was angry and decided to leave me alone. He pulled up his pants and walked out of my room. I stayed up that entire night. I had been sexually assaulted and no one– not even my mother–could protect me from this monster in the dark.

The assault went on for a few years. When I was 13, my mother spanked me for some infraction I cannot recall. Later, I was in my room and my brother came in to see me. I told him what my mother's husband had been doing to me over the years. I don't remember what my brother said to me, although I discovered later that evening that he had shared with my mother what I told him. I felt a sense of divine relief when she called me into her bedroom. But the relief was short-lived. Her husband was lying on the other side of the bed waiting to hear me repeat what I told my brother earlier that day!

I knew enough to know that she should have never confronted ME in front of him! When I repeated what I told my brother, her husband didn't flinch. He took a drag of his cigarette, shook his head and replied, "Now, you know better than that! You know I didn't do that to you! Why would you stand there and tell your mother that?!"

My mother she didn't raise her head to look at me one time. She just kept working the crossword puzzle in her lap. When she finally looked up, she told me to go back to my room. I was so hurt. I was in disbelief. I was ready to die. I had finally found the courage to tell my secret, only for it to mean nothing to the adults I depended on to protect me. My mother turned against her only daughter. She began blaming me for the negative parts of her marriage. She acknowledged that she believed my story, but she never asked him to leave.

While in high school, my friend who lived two doors away was heading out to church with her mom and dad, and I wanted to hang out with her. My mother gave me permission to go, and I was introduced to the place I have called my church home for the past 43 years. It was during these moments away that I gained new friends; a sense of belonging with other teens, and the nurturing that came with being in the presence of God. It was a small church with a small congregation, but I felt as though I could be myself in this environment. I was never forced to attend church, but here, I wanted to attend, because there were other teens who also attended. God pulled something out of me during this time – a willingness to serve Him. I joined the church, began singing in the choir, and participating in many youth activities. I was happy, if only for a few hours a week!

When I was 20 and unmarried, I got pregnant with my son. Three years later, I gave birth to another son. Single, with two sons and still living at home, with no money to speak of, my relationships with men were pretty much one-sided. I traded sex freely for love—or the illusion of it. It didn't matter that these brothers didn't care about me or my kids. I stopped caring about me. I stopped caring about my children. I stopped loving. I was a prisoner–locked up with two children I couldn't take care of without help. But in the midst of all of this, I had church. I had worship. I had God, and God had me!

I began to understand that God had not brought me this far to leave me. I asked God to use me for His will and years later, when God asked me, "Are you now ready to serve my people?" I answered, "Here I am, Lord; send me…"

On the last Sunday in December, 2002, I was ordained a deacon of my church–and I still serve faithfully to this day! I am saddened by the fact that during my childhood, I did not feel loved, needed or wanted. But I am not ashamed of who I was. I am not ashamed of where I was. I am not ashamed of my life. Instead, I am grateful that even in the midst of this painful life, I learned to rejoice and be glad in blessing the Lord at all times!

God has placed some good seeds in me, and I have made every effort to do right by Him and nurture those seeds so that they may produce good fruit.

I continue to discover who I am, to overcome my demons and to offer wisdom to those who struggle with their own identity and purpose.

My purpose is to extend God's love, even through my own suffering, so that God can be glorified. I thank God for the valleys I have crossed; I thank God for the mountains I have climbed; I thank God for granting me that sweet grace that is sufficient. I now realize that I am God's child and that God loves me in spite of me. I know that the bad things that happen to us do not have to mold us into something displeasing to Him. Situations can shape our faith and show us what it truly means to be forever grateful for His grace and mercy toward us!

This is my story, but it is not my life.

DONNA, CHICAGO, IL

Curled up in the farthest corner of a plaintiff's bench was a small, wiry, 10 year old girl with a boyish haircut, pink flowered turtleneck and corduroy jeans. She was very shy and wary, and people often forgot she was there when they spoke. She had just finished completing the most horrifying thing she had ever had to do—testify against her teacher for molesting her daily over the course of 8 months. Everyone was watching and staring—his friends and colleagues, lawyers and teacher's union reps, all siding with Mr. Sams to mitigate consequences, cast doubt, and deflect attention onto her.

As hard as cross-examination was, it did not prepare her for what she heard when she scooted out into the hall to get a sip of water to quench her persistent thirst.

"Just look at her! Who would ever want to touch that?!?"

"She looks like a mopy mop. I don't even know if she has any friends. That's why he offered to take her under his wing and give her special tutoring time---and this is the thanks he gets!"

"He is all the kids' favorite teacher! They are always coming out of his room with candy and can't wait to get to class."

Those were her other teachers. They did not take notice of her even when the soundless tears soaked the top cuff of her turtleneck. She had learned how to stay quiet, and she had for as long as she could. She didn't want anything bad to happen to her sisters if word got out of what happens during "tutoring." She didn't need tutoring anyway. She had already skipped a grade. But she liked spending time with the other misfit girls who, like her, came from the less entitled side of town. Plus, he only really bothered one of them at a time. Thankfully, her dad was a big man, a good Christian man who promised he would not get mad at her if she told him something that makes her feel very bad and small. He was big and strong enough to keep her sisters safe if she told, so she finally did.

It was a long climb out of the dark solitary hole for me. Going back to school among my peers, who missed that teacher and gave me dirty, accusing looks for forcing him to retire early. He denied everything. Even when two other girls gave similar testimony, he still lied. That part didn't bother me much, because I had my mother's words to comfort me: "Revenge is mine, saith the Lord. It doesn't say He needs any helpers."

God won that battle, too. The teacher died of throat cancer within two years of lying under oath.

So much attention was foisted upon me and as shy as I was, I didn't know how to process it all and still function socially. I read voraciously—the Bible, novels, non-fiction, anything I could get me hands on. I wrote poems and songs while trying to find some solace to drift into sleep. Finally, one night while praying in bed, I must have been in seventh grade, I felt God calling me out for being self-centered. I was shocked! I was so humble and unassuming, how could this be? Surely, I'm mistaken and not hearing Him right. The more I listened, the clearer the message became.

"Just because people were talking and whispering everywhere, does not mean they are talking about you! How self-important to think that you are the cause of all that focus. Maybe they are sad, and were hoping you would talk to them, but you were too wrapped up in your head to pay them any attention."

I mulled that over for a few days as I went about my normal routine, this time looking for evidence of anything pointing to me, the court case, or anything. I found nothing—not a scrap to hold onto. So, I let it go.

At a youth group retreat that month, I really let go and nudged myself out of my safe, solitary existence to speak up and speak out. The more I crept out of my comfort zone—holding back the tears, doubt and uncertainty in my throat and the vice of insecurity gripping my chest—the more I blossomed and grew. In my prayers each night, I bargained with God. It makes me chuckle now to think that I said, "Ok, God, I'm going to try it again tomorrow. If I'm going to put myself out there, you have to promise not to let them laugh." I did not think I could recover if I got shut down after putting myself out there like that. Because, at some point as God lures you further away from the things that are holding you back, you look ahead to His comfort and not behind, but that takes a lot of time—days, hours, minutes and seconds of holding your breath in faith. I spent my high school years with a few church youth group friends, working about 30 hours a week at a bridal shop, while planning my escape from low income farm life. I loved children. My parents had been foster parents for a time, and I babysat and cared for children as I grew up. God had truly transformed me. As my inner joy began exuding from every pore, the more beautiful I became to others. Many times, I heard the Ugly Duckling comparison.

I had a great family, but we were stressed by living paycheck to paycheck and getting free lunch, hand-me-downs, food stamps, and government cheese with gray powdered milk. My sisters weren't too ambitious. One was planning on getting married the month after she finished high school. Luckily, that was the motivation she needed to apply herself and try to bring her grades up to pass high school. God had touched her life, just in time to turn her around.

I was always very studious and saw education as my ticket out to move up in the world. After winning a high school science fair by discovering a new way to measure the molecular weight of alcohols, I applied to Ivy League schools and was waitlisted. Since that meant I would have to shoulder the bulk of the tuition burden when a spot came open, I decided to take a full scholarship to an almost Ivy League school's honor's program in Virginia.

Young, naïve and optimistic, I set out on my new adventure. I was an international relations major, because I excelled in Spanish and politics/debate and wanted to see the world. I was close to God but in a small personal way. I was overwhelmed with everything it had taken to get into a good college and apply for scholarships, working jobs to pay for relocating so far from home. A small part of me thought that I had already achieved something on my own.

Being gifted is fraught with its own challenges, and for me, the most important one was never having had to work at school before. A 17-year-old, 1,000 miles from home in an accelerated three-year dual major program, I got my first B (ever) in Honors Religion and Philosophy. I thought I had failed. I walked away from that scholarship and dropped out of school oh-so quietly, because I was too embarrassed to tell my parents. I moved about 50 miles away and started working and going to a community college to collect myself. In one semester I was awarded two associates degrees in chemistry and liberal arts for the work I completed.

That summer when I came home to visit, my folks asked how school was going. I replied, "Fine." I told them about going to Atlanta, and they casually mentioned that they knew I had dropped out. The school sent them withdrawal information, since I was a minor. Oh the laughs we had over that one!

Atlanta offered more opportunities, so I started working and going to Georgia State. I majored in criminal justice/pre-law and worked in law firms pursuing a legal career. I volunteered at my church in their children's ministry and taught seventh grade Sunday School. I felt compelled to make a difference in the lives of children. Toward the end of school, I did internships with the Gwinnett County District Attorney's Office-Child Protection Unit thinking that I was being faithful and following God's desire for my life as well as using my past to establish a connection or empathy with these victims.

I definitely made a difference. The investigations were compelling, and I attacked them with vigor, but after the second summer of working there,

I felt hollow and sad. These children's paths were sadly cast—a felony either by them or against them had put black marks on their future. So, I bided my time, finished my degree, while my own family grew and flourished. My oldest was about to begin kindergarten, and he was quite anxious about it.

One day, a friend called me and asked if I would consider a career in education. Never in a million years had I considered that because of the pain and damage I had experienced at the hands of one I had trusted in the same environment. I laughed, not because it was a crazy idea, but because I saw God's handiwork. He had used those quiet years to lay the framework for what he really wanted me to do. After a lot of prayer and wrestling with the Word, I agreed and proceeded toward a career in education.

Now, I make it my goal to empower and challenge all my students, and I do not accept less than their best. I have been awarded grants and honors for my work, Teacher of the Year, even, but my greatest glory comes from watching the flowers bloom. I try to be what others were not. Safe. Supporting. Accepting. Challenging. Encouraging. Visionary. Strong.

This is my story, but it is not my life.

BETH, BOSTON, MA

There is a ripple effect to an action. Here is mine...

I have always loved sports. I remember we were supposed to go to a Knicks game that night, but I only remember what my mind allows me to remember. I remember that I was always a curious child, something my mother encouraged in me from a very young age. I have no issue pushing the envelope to gain wisdom, understanding. Yet, there were certain questions I could never ask my mother. I was silent, but my actions toward her were filled with passionate anger because I believed what he said; I believed she knew.

My maternal grandmother was not born here, and she kept her culture alive. She taught my mother to keep family matters private. And my mother taught me that you keep things in the family, that you do not speak ill of the family. She believed that what happens at home stays at home; it was a rule we dared not break in order to protect the family name.

I was 10. He liked me. He liked basketball. I liked basketball, and I liked him. He bought me tickets to see the Knicks. At least, that is what he told me he did. We were going to the game. I thought we were going to the game. My mother told me I could go; she trusted him. He paid me attention, discussed things with me as if I were all grown up. I felt special. Before the game, we stopped at his friend's house to get something that would make the evening fun, he said.

I remember neither going to the game, nor the excuse I was probably told about why he forfeited the tickets he promised in exchange for watching the game on my grandmother's living room TV. He lived with her. He slept on her couch.

I sat in my panties and t-shirt, frightened; but I didn't know why. He told me he would make me a woman that night. I thought I should have been excited, but my body was shivering; something seemed off. I believed that the transformation from girl to woman should be amazing, but I was nervous, afraid. So he gave me something to calm my nerves. After what seemed like a couple of minutes, my vision was a little fuzzy. I remember opening my eyes seeing the top of his head between my legs, moving very fast. Even the thought of him spitting on me with his mouth was gross. I pushed his head away hard, and he fell back on the floor. If this was part of the transformation into womanhood, I didn't want it.

He said my mother had okayed this transformation, but he cautioned me that part of the game was she would act like she didn't know, and I could never ask her about this. But if Mommy said, it was ok, why didn't it feel ok? Why couldn't we talk about it? Shots at the doctor didn't feel ok, but Mommy always talked about those things to me. Why was this different?

I don't remember much of what he said during this time. I remember my body felt heavy and very slow to move. He tried to put his "thing" there. But it would not fit. It hurt, and I pushed him off of me. I scratched his leg and left a deep gash as evidence of my rejection of him. I told him "No! I don't want to do this anymore."

How could this be? I was shaking. I went into my grandmother's room and feigned being tired. I was confused and overwhelmed with emotion. Now what? Morning couldn't come fast enough. All I wanted was to be was with my mommy. I wanted to be Mommy's little girl again. But what could I say to her? He told me if I told her, he would do it again and that not doing it right the first time would disappoint her.

The Impact...

I was frightened, and I did not know what to do. She wanted this? She knew about this? How? Why? That Bitch! She knew! Everyone knew? Everyone went through this with him? Everyone else liked this, and this was how you become a woman? How could this be true? The anger was born, and the memory of that day was locked away.

For the next two years, I gave my mother a hell I wish on no one. I acted out, smart mouthed her, threw things. I was labeled a "troubled child". But I was actually misunderstood and confused. Who could I trust? Who really loved me?

I wanted to run away, and when I was 12 years old, I escaped to my best friend's house. Her mother and my mother were friends and our grandmothers were friends too, but somehow I thought my family wouldn't find me. When they did, I had to return home. And then the interrogation began. My father told me a fake story about how I was "spotted on the roof of a building with some boy, and I needed to go to the doctor because they wanted to find out if I was a virgin or not." I was a virgin. I mean, I had never been with a boy, but I had been "with" my uncle. I trusted him; he was family. So when he told me Mommy said it was ok, I believed him. I felt betrayed by my mother and frightened by my father's interrogation, so I told what my then 40-year-old uncle did to me. I went back two years in my memory bank and unlocked the truth.

I believed my dad loved me. I believed my dad would protect me. He told me he loved me more than life itself. For sure, he would take care of this. My dad told me he would kill him. I actually wanted that to happen. I was excited. I felt protected. I felt loved.

I never realized how the 10-year-old girl in me was impacted by this one day. I became confused by love. I didn't understand what love was. From that point on, I always felt dirty. I constantly cleaned myself. My dad always would tell me, "I love you more than life itself." I don't understand what that means. I still can't reconcile love with a failure to protect.

There are a few things I do understand. I understand that when I got married at 18, I married to escape the house. I understand that when I had my first child at 19, I did it because I didn't know how to love myself. I wanted to love someone else. I understand the birth of my second child at 20, was so my first would have someone to love and protect her. When I wanted to kill myself at 21 and couldn't, I now understand that was God loving me. And when I divorced at 40, I know it was because I needed to love myself. For once, I needed to do it for me. For so long, I claimed to love with fluidity, but I couldn't define love.

I was raised Catholic, so I knew tradition. I respected the existence of God. Today, I understand the relationship of God. Today, I am a Christian. The day I wanted to kill myself, I was stopped in my tracks by the sight of two little babies curled up in bed. The next day, my neighbor invited me to go to church with her the following Sunday. I went, and I had never experienced anything like it. People hugged, sang and cried. I was overwhelmed. I had never experienced love like that.

The preacher was talking to me! That very day, I ran down the aisle to give my life to Christ. And since then, my life has not been the same. Many had claimed to love me, but this was different. God loved me as I was; not for what I did or didn't do; not because of what I accomplished or created. He saw me where I was—broken and abused. I didn't know that my dad's version of loving me more than life itself would translate into the real love I found when I read of God's love in John 3:16.

I now know that my uncle's transgressions could have been more devastating for me. I could have run away to the streets, instead of to my best friend's house. I could have been an addict in many forms…but God. God sustained me as I learned to deal with the pain of that one moment. God kept me and loved me through the years. God is teaching me more and more how to love and how to forgive. My uncle died of lung cancer nearly 25 years after the molestation. I forgave him, because he was warped. I forgave my mother for not saving me from what she knew nothing of. I am learning to forgive my dad, because it is necessary. I am learning to love; deeply and fully because God loves me. I know that in the act of forgiving, I am healing, and in healing, I am learning to love even more. Most importantly I know I cannot do any of this without God. The transformation my uncle promised me was twisted and perverted. But I am transforming daily – growing in love, in God and in my service to the world.

It is receiving that sustained me then and keeps me now. I am closer to Christ than I ever imagined I could be.

This is the ripple effect of that one moment.

This is my story, but it is not my life.

KHAN-YIN, QUEENS, NY

"How many men have you been with?" he asked. Wow, I thought. I had never been asked that before. How many men had I been with? And are we talking just men? Because the guys I had been with in high school hardly qualify as men. And what about the girl I met online and experimented with. And what exactly does "been with" mean? Is he using the Bill Clinton definition, or do all sexual encounters count? And if you really want to get technical, should I include consensual and nonconsensual acts? How exactly did he expect me to answer that question? It's not that straightforward for a woman like me... so I declined to answer.

You see, my first sexual encounter happened around age 6. The details are sketchy, but I do remember the room–blue curtains, bunk beds with superhero sheets, Connect4 and Monopoly on the dresser. That's how I've been able to determine approximately how old I was. I know my aunt lived in this particular house during the early years of my life. Unlike the first encounter, the last encounter with my molester is very clear, I remember it like a movie I've seen a hundred times and can recite all the lines. That night, he said, "I'm sorry, I won't do this again." And he didn't. I was 12 years old. From the very first time he touched me and made me touch him, I became numb. I can't even tell you today how I felt in those moments, because I just didn't feel anything; it was almost like an out-of-body experience.

Honestly, I don't even remember much about anything that went on during those years. Some therapists believe victims of tragedy sometimes block out memories to avoid the pain. So, perhaps that's the case. Having that experience, along with not having a father around as I grew up, and no models for healthy family relationships, I would spend many years lost; seeking to fill a void I didn't even know I had.

"Say your grace before you eat." That's what my mom would say. At 16, I was feeling out of control on the inside but trying to maintain the appearance of control on the outside. I wasn't praying to a God who ignored my cries. I doubted His existence, because He sure hadn't been around in a long time from what I could tell. Where was he when my little brother died? Where was he when my father went to prison? Where was he all those years I was being molested? Where was he when my mom needed help with food and bills? Where was he? No grace for me. I rejected the thought that there was a God. I began being many mothers' nightmare daughter: that sneaky, promiscuous, lying teen that appears to be doing alright in the light, but behind closed doors was unrecognizable. My mom walked in on me having sex in the living room of our home. She was furious, and she waited until the next day to attempt to talk to me sensibly. When she did speak, I could not hold it together; I cried hysterically and told her nobody understood my pain. I confessed to her that I had been molested many times over the years by my older cousin, Jeffery. I was not sure if my mom initially believed me, a fear many victims face. She called her sister, his mother, and told her about it. And when they asked him about it, he admitted it. My mom hung up the phone and asked if I wanted to send him to jail. At the time, I didn't want to bring any more attention to this situation. Later that week, he apologized to my mom, gave her some money, and that was the end of it. Case closed. No consequences or punishment. I didn't realize it then, but this became the source of tremendous resentment toward my mother and my aunt for many years. This is also the time I started seriously considering suicide, a thought I had contemplated since eighth grade. What did I have to live for? I felt worthless, but I had no idea why.

Unable to figure out how to pay for college, I decided to enlist in the Army. I would be able to leave home, try to get a fresh start, and give my mom the financial relief of having one less mouth to feed. In Fort Jackson, South Carolina, basic training was rough, but I did it! I think I cried more in two months than I had in the past two years! Basic training was the first time as a young adult that I realized there are some things I would not be able to do on my own, things that would take some supernatural strength to get me through. Most people went to church every Sunday just to get away from the drill sergeants and to interact with the opposite sex. In the non-denominational service lead by an Army chaplain, I found myself willingly praying to the God I felt had forgotten about me. I was lonely, unsure, emotionally drained, and I didn't have any friends or family to lean on. I needed Him. In those moments of prayer, I felt comforted and calm, as if all was going to be okay. This is just temporary; I began to believe. The hell of Basic Training would not be my eternity, although it often felt like it.

While in the Army I discovered that there were other women who had experienced sexual abuse. In fact, there were so many women that there were support groups that we were encouraged to attend. It was during a support group session that I first shared my childhood experiences with anyone other than my mom. The support group was helpful for a while, but I stopped attending those meetings when the stigma began to weigh heavily on me. The victim's club was not something I wanted a membership in. After I stopped attending the support group, my promiscuous behavior resurfaced. Once again, I was trying to fill the black hole in my soul. Once again, it didn't work.

While in the Army, I met a guy, who loved me so much that he asked me to marry him. Marriage was something new to me. My mom never married, so I thought my own marriage was my opportunity to change my life. I said yes and after knowing each other only six months, we got married in a judge's chambers in Tacoma, Washington. I was 19 years old and, unknowingly, beginning 13 unstable years.

There were some good times and some great times, like the birth of our two beautiful children. But from my viewpoint, there were far fewer good times that bad ones. There was a lot of infidelity, mostly committed by me. Divorce was the topic of discussion every few months. I made numerous suicide threats and actually attempted suicide a couple of times. I took pills and was admitted to the hospital twice during these years. I desperately needed a savior; life was exhausting physically and emotionally. I felt hopeless and ashamed. Who was I?

In 2009, I made up my mind to end the marriage. It took a few months for me to muster the courage to ask for a divorce, but in early 2010, I did it. I believe my ex-husband still hates me, because he put up with so much of my mess before I gave up. I was a mess, a walking ball of depression, blaming everything wrong with my life on someone else. I was in the lowest place I had ever been, and I asked God for a mulligan, a do-over. I didn't deserve it, but I promised God I would do better the next time around. I promised him I would learn to have faith, but I needed a guide, because I just didn't know where to begin.

While going through my divorce, I began dating my current husband, a man who, in spite of his own flaws, is full of faith. He became my guide. We married quickly, a little too quickly to some. But we wanted to do things the right way, God's way. We didn't want to be the couple that was shacking up and having premarital sex while attending church together every Sunday, so we moved quickly, marrying just three months after my divorce was final. After a certain age, it doesn't take long to know if the other person is someone you can live the rest of your life with. I wasn't 19 years old this time around. And between the two of us, we had five kids for whom we needed to set good examples.

Going to church on a regular basis was new for me, but I began to enjoy it. Over the years, I occasionally had gone to church when I felt desperation in my spirit but never anything close to regular since I first joined the Army. My husband was Catholic, and that too was new for me. I had so many questions, and being a "cradle" Catholic, he had so few answers. He just grew up believing, never questioning what his parents had instilled in him. After a year of marriage, the time came when I decided I wanted to convert to Catholicism and officially join the Church.

I spent the next three years evolving spiritually. It wasn't easy, and my journey isn't over. But my narrow lens is now wide, and I lean on God daily, not just in those times of desperation. I came to the realization that I am bigger than my problems, and I recognize the blessings—not just the curses—in my life. So many times, I wanted to take my own life, but God had other plans for me. I am still searching for my true purpose and trying as best I can to understand that all experiences have molded and shaped me into the woman I am today.

It has taken years for me to understand that not dealing with pain only buries it temporarily; it eventually resurfaces. Recently, I sought therapy and spent months in an outpatient program to take ownership of my life and gain the tools I needed to manage in moments when my wounds reopen. Forgiveness of others and forgiveness of me was the key to rid myself of guilt and shame. Today, I am a better wife, a better mother, a better friend, a better daughter, and, most importantly, a better servant of God. My black hole has been filled.

I hope that my story inspires others never to settle for less than what God expects of us.

This is my story, but it is not my life.

RONNE, POWDER SPRINGS, GA

My parents were at Wednesday night Bible class. I called and got no answer. Fortunately, my aunt lived next door to the church. My cousin, Emmanuel, answered. I asked, "Can you go next door to the church and tell my mom to call me? Hurry up!"

"What's wrong?" he asked.

I didn't have time to explain. "Hurry! I might be dying."

To this day, I have no idea how I got to the hospital. Perhaps by ambulance. Perhaps, my parents came to get me. I don't know. My next memory was waking up from surgery with my mom, my uncle, who was the pastor of the church, and a policeman staring at me. I still don't know why my dad wasn't there as well.

"Do you feel like talking? I need to ask you some questions. Who did this to you?" the police officer asked.

Hell no, I thought. I don't feel like talking.

I wanted to disappear. The looks on their faces made me wish I had died. I wanted to be left alone. I refused to talk about what happened, and I never uttered a word about it until five years later. My mom never pushed, but occasionally, when I would let my anger get the best of me, she would say, "Maybe you need to talk about it." She protected me fiercely. She tried to absorb my pain. She was always there.

It was December, 1981. My parents had gone to church. My two older sisters were with them. My younger brother, baby sister, and I had stayed home. My brother had gone to a friend's house. I think my sister was asleep.

I was watching television when the sliding door to the patio began to move. I jumped, but was relieved to see it was my neighbor, Mr. White. When he asked me to come outside, I went. There was snow on the ground; a rarity in Mississippi. He started to kiss me, and I was repulsed. He became angry and knocked me to the ground. The cold snow was on my back. I was violently shivering, and he kept trying to force himself inside me. I moved quickly and accidentally kneed him where it hurt. He hit me. I spit at him. Seconds later, I felt the knife cutting my insides. He said if I told, he would do the same to my sister. I was in so much pain. The burning sensation was unimaginable. Blood was everywhere. I crawled inside to the phone and called for help. I didn't know how I would explain it, but his secret was safe.

He lived right across the street, so for years, I watched that son of a bitch smirk. He winked at times. It didn't matter. When I could, I was going to kill him. I'd make him suffer like he made me suffer. I had no clue how I would do it, but it would be slow and would include a knife. He would most certainly pay.

I was lying in the hospital damn near dead following a molestation, and I learned that my first boyfriend was lying on me, telling everyone that he had taken my virginity. When I returned to school after the Christmas break, everybody was staring at me. How could he do that to me? Friend and foe alike ridiculed me. My best friend made a melody about me getting my cherry popped. They all sang it. I was the laughing stock of my school, and he was boasting just as if he was proudly responsible for my near-death experience.

Of course, he had no clue what really happened, but apparently enough had been said that he related his lies to it. I'm sure my siblings surmised from the blood that soaked the carpet and my visible, guarded pain that something sex-related happened. Someone had talked, but it sure wasn't me.

What angered me more than anything was my former boyfriend gave my attacker a get-out-of-jail free card. The sick pedophile was off the hook because my own boyfriend was taking responsibility for hurting me. I didn't know how Mr. White was going to be arrested, indicted, prosecuted and sent away for life, but I intended to find a way. I was angry. It was on!

Whenever I had an audience, I held court. My tongue was worse than any weapon, and when I bested my opponents, the spectators laughed – hard, and I felt vindicated. My tongue became my sword, always sharp, always quick. I couldn't fight with my fists, but anyone who ever crossed me wished I had hit them.

That's how I coped. For years, I would say I was not affected by molestation like others were. I overcame. It made me who I am. I was strong and would never be taken advantage of. I excelled at most things. I have never started a fight in my life of any kind. I have never been in a physical fight with anyone other than my brother, but boy could I cut you like a knife with my tongue. At times, I would take pride in my weapon. She was beautiful, sardonic, meticulous, and cut with precision. Every time someone said, "You don't want to mess with her," my chest puffed up, and if anyone challenged me, the verbal victory was more delectable than the choicest cut of meat.

I raised my sons never to be mean to anyone. I despised mean people. If they were unkind, I would spank them. Deep down, I am kind, but I excused mistreating people who mistreated me, because I thought they deserved it. I gave myself a pass, because I only finished what others started.

Ironically, I took pride in cutting people with my tongue. I haven't completely stopped. Whenever my heart is pierced or my ego is bruised, the pain is palpable, and I go for it. I didn't become suicidal or promiscuous. I've always loved myself, and my family is great so I never needed to look for love in the wrong places. I didn't need therapy to survive. I didn't have nightmares or even give it much thought. I thought I was happy and whole, but wholeness doesn't take pride in cutting people. I wasn't okay. I was simply successful in hiding my scars.

I don't know why she never pushed, but my mom was right. Maybe I needed to talk about it.

I have been covered my entire life through the prayers of the righteous. It is the only way I have survived. I know God's word. I spent a minimum of three days a week in church until I left for college. I can recall many sermons about the power of the words we speak. I can recite the scriptures. *"Death and life are in the power of the tongue." "But those things which proceed out of the mouth come from the heart, and they defile a man." "There is one who speak like the piercings of a sword, but the tongue of the wise promotes health." "Do you see a man hasty in his words? There is more hope for a fool than for him."* But, of course, they didn't apply to me. I had been violated. It was brutal. I was justified.

"For out of the abundance of the heart the mouth speaks." There it was— God rebuking me. I was staunchly defending why someone was deserving of my crafty tongue-lashing while at the same time talking about my abhorrence of mean-spirited people and my kindness. God spoke through a wise old woman who was eavesdropping and interjected with the scripture that pierced me. She followed with, "And whatever you do, whether in word or deed, do it all in the name of the Lord Jesus."

I thought I was living a life of kindness, love, and compassion. I was teaching it and being a hypocrite. I would like to say I was hurting my transgressors unknowingly, but I know better. My tongue was acerbic, hateful and destructive.

The Bible speaks to every situation, and anyone connected to God knows He talks to us all day. I don't profess to be cured. I'm clearly a work in progress, but my prayer is fervent:

33 Teach me, O LORD, the way of Your statutes,
And I shall keep it to the end.
34 Give me understanding, and I shall keep Your law;
Indeed, I shall observe it with my whole heart.
35 Make me walk in the path of Your commandments,
For I delight in it.
36 Incline my heart to Your testimonies,
And not to covetousness.
37 Turn away my eyes from looking at worthless things,
And revive me in Your way.
38 Establish Your word to Your servant,
Who is devoted to fearing You.
39 Turn away my reproach which I dread,
For Your judgments are good.
40 Behold, I long for Your precepts;
Revive me in Your righteousness.

Mr. White changed my life. I became a bitter person. He was never held responsible, and I do not know what happened to him. When I spoke of killing him, I was reminded that vengeance is the Lord's. I am sure it was exacted precisely. I do still hope it was slow and painful. Roger, the former boyfriend who caused me so much pain and embarrassment, was as young as me at the time. He did not know any better. Years later, he apologized, and I forgave him.

Let the words of my mouth, and the meditation of my heart, be acceptable in thy sight, O Lord, my strength, and my redeemer. Amen.

This is my story, but it is not my life.

MONIQUE, JACKSON, MS

ILLNESS

I have four siblings—three sisters and a brother. I was raised in a Catholic Christian home where I knew of God, believed in God, but did not have a relationship with God. I attended church services, but I never got involved. When I married my Baptist husband, we attended our Baptist church, but continued basically to be uninvolved. One day, however, while our family played in a local park, we met a couple that assisted God in lifting the veil from my eyes. They invited us to dinner one evening, and as we talked—man-to-man and woman-to woman—God's word was shared. I was convicted. I realized that although I believed in God, I did not have a relationship with Him; I did not know him. From there, I eased into learning more about Him. I started attending Sunday school, Precept classes and volunteering at church. That is also when Satan started attacking me, and my faith began to be tested.

One morning, as I put my feet on the floor, pain radiated through the bottom of both of my feet. Eventually, lethargy accompanied the pain. I used to be a person who walked and hiked hills and mountains. Now, I could hardly walk across the room without pain. I sought out my doctor who drew blood, then I had to wait for an answer. One evening after work I was waiting in a lobby while my daughter was attending her piano lesson. My phone rang. It was my doctor, and at the six o'clock hour, I figured it couldn't be good.

She explained to me that I had an autoimmune disease. I didn't understand what that meant, but I read everything I could put my hands on. I learned that my body was attacking itself. My joints were inflamed; my muscles hurt; I had ulcers in my mouth; and my white blood count was abnormally low. I had multiple symptoms, but she couldn't yet pinpoint a diagnosis. She called it Undifferentiated Connective Tissue Disorder. I was given plenty of medication to get it under control, including steroids that made me gain weight and feel miserable, but the pain eased up and life moved on. My husband worked out with me and once again I began to walk, a hundred feet, then a block, and finally a mile. I began to get my proverbial footing on life again. I had gained 30 pounds from the medication; I joined a support group and began to take the pounds off week by week. I had kept this journey to myself and my family. I didn't share my pain with anyone but family. Then God spoke to me through people in my Sunday school class, He told me that I was depriving others from praying with me and praying for me. I shared my story and started gaining my self-esteem and strength back through prayer and encouragement.

Little did I know I was to be challenged again, that I would need the strength of my Lord and Savior. Have you ever felt like Job? Like trouble was raining down on you? One problem after another and I never uttered, Why me, Lord? Because I knew the answer: Why not me! Who was I? I was susceptible to sin and Satan just like everyone else.

I was sitting on the side of the bed watching TV, when a program about breast cancer came on. The host said you should examine your breasts once a month. So while I was sitting there I started rubbing in a circular motion on each breast. I started with the right and found nothing; I didn't expect to. Then I began to do the same thing on the left side and found a lump. I did it again and found it again. I thought, Now what do I do? I was worried. It was December, and I had changed my insurance plan at work in November; my new plan started January 1. I thought, "This is going to have to wait until my new plan starts and I can find a new doctor. He can't do any do anything about it and neither can I until next month. Why ruin Christmas?" So I waited and hoped the lump would just go away. It didn't.

In January, I searched for a new doctor and found one nearby. I was nervous when I entered the office but was immediately at ease once I walked in the door. A friend from church worked in the office and greeted me warmly. She made me comfortable and introduced me to my new doctor. I was examined; had an ultrasound and referred to an oncologist. God placed me in great hands. Dr. J is a sought-after doctor; her waiting room was 30 people deep. She is the best. Dr. J called my husband and me into her office and closed the door. She had reviewed my test results and began to walk us through my possible diagnosis; she drew us pictures to illustrate my lump and what needed to be done. She explained the next steps in my journey, trying to suppress our fears. My husband's words still resonate in my mind; "Will she survive this? Is she going to live?" Dr. J said my chances of a complete recovery were good.

Dr. J referred me to a surgeon who was to remove my tumor. He would send it off for testing to determine what type of breast cancer I would be fighting. He scheduled me for an outpatient biopsy. I can still visualize and smell the procedure. The day of the procedure, I lay on a table with a drape partially over my chest and a cover between me and a clear view of my surgeon. He numbed up my breast tissue and began to cut me open. He used a cauterizing procedure to reduce the bleeding. I could clearly smell burning flesh, my flesh. My surgeon was very personable and relatable, and he talked to me throughout the procedure, telling exactly what he was doing. He said he could perform just the biopsy or remove the entire 1.5 centimeter lump. I voted to remove the entire lump; I wanted it out of me. Next, came the waiting.

A week later, my surgeon called me back to his office to inform me of my prognosis. I had Triple Negative Breast Cancer. There are generally three receptors or factors that fuel the growth of breast cancer: estrogen, progesterone and HER2 (or Human Epidermal Growth factor receptors). These are what most cancer drugs are developed to treat. I had triple negative breast cancer; which means the traditional treatments are not effective. It responds to chemotherapy, but is considered aggressive and more likely to recur than other breast cancers. I needed to go back under the knife, this time under anesthesia to remove additional tissue and to take out a few lymph nodes under my arm near the tumor to test them for cancer. I was at peace, but my husband was worried enough for both of us.

When I awoke, my arm and breast were in a lot of pain and I was told that he found a second tumor. The two combined were more than two centimeters, making chemotherapy a necessity and radiation possible.

It was time to see Dr. J again and learn more about my new journey. Every office visit meant lab work before seeing Dr. J. My first lab test showed my white blood count was already too low for my first chemo treatment. My autoimmune disease was making it difficult for me to effectively battle my breast cancer. My plan of action was to have six sessions of my chemotherapy cocktail over a period of four months, followed up by seven weeks of radiation for five days a week. During this entire process, I continued to work. I had chemo treatments on Thursdays, stayed home and recuperated Friday through Sunday and went back to work on Monday.

I had more downs than ups. We constantly fought to keep my white count up and my platelets at a normal level to continue with my therapy; if they weren't up, chemo would have to be delayed, and my treatment would take that much longer to be completed. One day during a week off from chemo, I thought I was feeling pretty well. I completed my labs and was waiting to see Dr. J. My labs were running behind and were not completed by the time my office visit concluded, so I was about to leave when someone came running down the hall after me.

"Stop you can't go yet. You need to be admitted to the hospital for a blood transfusion; your platelets are dangerously low." If I had been bumped or cut, I could have bled to death, but God saved me once again.

My chemo treatments started in May and successfully concluded in October of that year. In January, I started my radiation, which I thought would be the easy part. I had to lie still and be naked from the waist up 5 days a week while a machine pushed radiation into my chest. It made me tired, browned my skin like a dark suntan but strangely made me comfortable with my nakedness. It was almost over, or so I thought.

I continued to visit Dr. J on a monthly basis to get my blood tested to verify the cancer had not returned. We celebrated the completion of my treatments with a family vacation in June. Life was starting to get back to normal.

In November, I came down with a fever and sinus infection that just would not go away with over the counter medicine. I made an appointment with my internist and she confirmed that I had a sinus infection and prescribed antibiotics for 10 days. I completed them and did not get better. I returned to the doctor who extended my antibiotics another 10 days and ran blood tests to be safe. I was at an early Christmas lunch with staff when my phone rang; it was Dr. J. I thought to myself, Why is she calling me?

She explained that my internist shared my blood work with her. I had Acute Myeloid Leukemia–a cancer of the blood and bone marrow. She wanted me in the hospital immediately. My thoughts were jumbled. I had to wrap things up at work and tell my boss. I needed to talk to my employees. I told Dr. J I would see her on Monday, no sooner.

My world was once again turned upside down. I had gone to the restroom to take the call in private. When I returned to the table, I explained to my team that I had cancer. I would be away from work throughout my treatment. I didn't know how long it would take. I managed to drive back to the office and call my husband; I told him the little I knew or understood. I had had less than a one percent chance of getting leukemia from the chemotherapy treatments.

I called my boss and explained what I knew to him before telling the rest of my co-workers. I could barely get the words out. I was trembling, but the words came out, and I continued to put one foot in front of the other. As the day went on, I shared the story once more with my family, then with my church family and prepared to be admitted to the hospital. I got on the computer to learn everything I could about leukemia; it was not promising. But I had my family, my friends, my co-workers and church members praying with me to God for my healing.

After I was admitted, they started my chemotherapy regimen. I received chemotherapy around the clock for five days in an attempt to put the leukemia into remission. The treatment wiped out my immune system. I was to stay in my hospital room for six weeks, getting out of bed only with assistance. I celebrated Christmas and then the new year there. If I fell or bumped into anything I was told I could bleed out because my platelets were too low that my blood couldn't clot.

I asked my doctors daily, "When are you going to let me go home?" I received encouragement from friends and family through cards, phone calls and visits. The nurses were amazed that my four walls were covered in cards. I knew God loved me and so did my extended family and friends.

I was released in January only to be told I'd have to come back in February for more chemo treatments. I was referred to a new doctor, Dr. B, a bone marrow transplant specialist who informed me and my husband that my Leukemia could not be cured or kept in check with chemotherapy. I needed a donor for a bone marrow or stem cell transplant. I would die without it.

Donors are not easy to find, and it was thought that finding a match for me would be difficult. Siblings have only 25 percent chance of matching. I told my sisters of the dilemma, and they all agreed to be tested. My baby sister announced that she would be my match, she would be my donor. And she was a perfect match. God had plans for me; he was not done with me.

The transplant was scheduled for March, but first I had to see a cardiologist to ensure my heart was capable of withstanding additional chemotherapy. They scheduled me for an echocardiogram, a heart ultrasound. After the test, I visited with the doctor and got more bad news: my breast cancer chemotherapy treatments damaged my heart, and I could not withstand additional chemotherapy.

I said, "I don't understand. If you determine I can't have more chemo, I can't have a bone marrow transplant to get rid of the Leukemia. What am I supposed to do now?" I left his office despondent and in tears. I got into my car, crying and calling out to God in a loud voice. "What am I to do now God? You got me this far, what now?" My phone rang at that very moment; it was my cardiologist. He had spoken to my transplant doctor, and they had come up with a new game plan just for me. They were going to change my chemotherapy drug that had not previously been used for transplants but that was known not to have side effects to the heart. They planned to use a lower dosage that would kill off my cells and allow my sister's bone marrow to take over. I hung up the phone and praised God and thanked him for saving me once again.

The next week, I completed my chemotherapy followed by my stem cell transplant donated by my youngest sister. Each day was a struggle: blood tests, drugs and IVs. For 120 days I saw no one but my family and the medical team at my doctor's office. But within six months, with God's strength and healing, I had recuperated. I was free from cancer and could go on with my journey. I am God's walking miracle, a living testimony of His grace and mercy.

This is my story, but it is not my life.

LISA, ATLANTA, GA

I stood in the corner of the small neo-natal intensive care unit (NICU) watching the doctor run a tiny scope across my newborn son's chest. I realized that my eight-pound baby boy, who was delivered amid the fanfare of Independence Day the previous night, might not be as healthy as was originally thought. Initially the pediatrician's decision to request that a cardiologist come to the hospital to examine Paul was presented as just a precaution. But as the doctor painstakingly examined my baby for what seemed like an eternity, I realized that something was wrong. The doctor introduced himself and said, "Your son has a congenital heart defect." I had no idea what that meant. But when he told me that my precious baby boy would require open-heart surgery, I was numb all over. I felt as though I had been enveloped by something inexplicably warm.

Over the ensuing weeks, everything that happened felt like reality TV starring us. My husband arrived about the same time as the special ambulance that had been summoned to carefully transport our son to Fairfax Hospital for Children, where the surgery would take place. When they rolled Paul out to the ambulance, the weight of what was happening hit me like a ton of bricks. I immediately checked myself out of the hospital; there was no way I was staying another minute there without him. Having had a C-section, I still required medical care, but the other hospital could not accommodate me. I got in the car and cried. I entered the hospital expecting a routine delivery, but nothing was turning out the way I had expected it to.

How had we gotten here? After his birth, the staff cleaned and checked the baby, and assigned us to a private room. I held him and dedicated my little one to God. I never suspected that anything was wrong. But the next day, the nurse kept coming into our room. As a second-time mom, I sensed that she was coming in way too much. Finally, I asked her why she was checking on the baby so much. She told me that while he seemed healthy, she sensed something was wrong. When her shift ended, she would be off for three days and she would be worried that something wasn't right. She asked permission to take him down to the NICU to have him checked out by the neonatologist. I agreed to allow her to take him. Florie returned 15 minutes later and informed me that Paul was breathing at less than 50%, so he had to stay in the NICU. I visited Paul at the NICU, and the neonatologist assured me that it was not a big deal. He also assured me that I would be taking my son home the next day. Our pediatrician called in a cardiologist as a precaution and informed us that she would not release Paul until they confirmed that everything was all right. Later, we learned that if Paul had gone home, he probably would have died in his sleep from sudden infant death syndrome (SIDS). I will always consider Nurse Florie and Dr. Kunkel to be Paul's personal angels.

We met the surgeon Dr. Bechara Akl, founder of the pediatric cardiac surgery program at Inova Fairfax Hospital for Children. He patiently explained Paul's congenital heart defect (CHD) and what he would have to do to repair the problem. Many people are familiar with birth defects such as cerebral palsy and Down's Syndrome, but most are surprised to discover that CHDs are the number one birth defect. The American Heart Association considers CHDs a structural problem with the heart present at birth. One in every 100 babies is born with a CHD; of those one in 10 is a fatal defect. Congenital heart defects occur at least three times more often than childhood cancers. The mortality rate for these children may be as high as 50 percent, depending on the condition.

To our surprise, Dr. Akl informed us that we had to wait about a week for Paul's surgery. Since Paul was a newborn and he would be unconscious for an unspecified amount of time following his surgery, they wanted to make sure his body would remember how to function outside of the womb. Every day for the next week, I spent the entire day at the hospital sitting by Paul's isolette. Having a baby in the NICU was like nothing I could have ever imagined. As I looked around, I saw that my baby was a giant compared to the other newborns there. I learned that the majority of the babies had been born prematurely, some weighing only a few pounds. Many of the other moms tried to figure out how a baby the size of Paul was in the NICU. Those conversations were my opportunity to share my faith—and to remind myself that God was not wasting my trial. I was amazed by how He used me to encourage other mothers with sick babies. I always had my Bible and my journal with me. I talked with them and told them I was praying for their infants.

Paul's surgery was Friday, the thirteenth, and I was in a daze so the significance of the day was lost on me. Dr. Akl said that the surgery could take up to 12 hours, including prep-time. I was eerily calm, feeling as though I had fallen into routine in the nine days of Paul's time on earth. My church members, same as people country-wide, were praying for Paul, who I had held only twice because he was hooked up to so many machines in the NICU. I held him once more before he was wheeled into the operating room. When my parents commented on how amazed they were with how I was handling the pressure, I explained that God's peace was with me. I believed God was using the situation for His glory and that He would heal my son.

When the surgery was finally over, Dr. Akl told us everything went well, with one potential complication. The team discovered that the upper left lobe of Paul's lung had not fully developed. There was no blood flowing to that side. He assured us that Paul could lead a normal life with one lung and that there was still hope the lobe might still develop. Paul was in a special room in the pediatric intensive care unit (PICU). His chest cavity was open to keep the pressure that had built up around his heart from getting worse, so he was sedated for the next three days. He was hooked up to so many machines that the beeps created their own music. Monday, if all went well, they would close his chest up, and then Paul's recovery would begin.

I spent every day at the hospital, and I continued my ministry of encouragement. I met a woman whose son had drowned. We spent time together sitting in a special waiting room right next to the PICU. I prayed for her and encouraged her, and we talked a lot about the healing power of Jesus. Her son's condition was critical, and she was incredibly sad and afraid. Everywhere I turned, there were hurting women in need of encouragement or just a friendly face and a kind word. I was happy to provide it. It definitely forced me to keep my eyes on God instead of my circumstances.

On Monday, Dr. Akl closed Paul's chest and took him off of all of the sedatives, but he didn't wake up. Every day, I sat by the bed, holding his tiny little hand and singing songs to him and praying repeatedly that God would open Paul's eyes. It was especially difficult when the doctors made their twice-a-day rounds, commenting, "Wow, the little guy still hasn't awakened." Wednesday, they decided that a test to confirm normal brain activity was in order.

"Lord," I prayed, "I thought you told me that you were going to heal my son." I thought about the man who came to Jesus and asked him to heal his daughter. Jesus asked him if he believed. He said he believed, but he also asked God for more faith. So I prayed and told God that I needed more faith.

The tests showed normal brain activity. Paul, the doctors said, would wake up when he was ready. I realized that I had to keep praying and wait on God's timing. I kept visiting the NICU lactation room. I encouraged the new moms there, and each day, I spent time with the woman who hoped and prayed that her son, the drowning victim, would awaken from a coma.

On Friday of that week, I was on the verge of tears as I got off the elevator on the PICU floor to visit Paul. I decided to just pray and focus on God's goodness instead of my rocky emotions. I started to feel calmer as I walked along the corridor.

As I turned the corner, I heard a hoarse cry coming from the end of the hall. I recognized that voice anywhere. Paul had awakened.

As I drew closer, I saw that the rails were raised around the bed. My heart beat out of control in my chest. Paul was awake. I longed to hold him, but he was still hooked up to several machines. Later that night, holding my precious son in my arms was like a gift. All the praise went to my Father in heaven. I thanked Him for all the people He used to heal my son. It was indeed a miracle.

Paul's condition quickly improved. Two days after he awakened, they removed the feeding tube, the big I.V. lines from his left shoulder and the extra oxygen. The next day, Paul moved to a private room. The doctors were pleased with his progress. I longed to take my baby home, but no one had told me when that would happen. Three days later, however, my dream came true: I took my baby home from the hospital. There would be follow-up appointments with the pediatrician, surgeon and cardiologist, but he wasn't hooked up to any monitors, and he wasn't on any medication.

The first night Paul was home, I was worried about going to sleep. What if something happens while I was sleeping? There wouldn't be a machine to tell me if he had problems breathing. I remembered dedicating Paul to the Lord shortly after his birth. I told God that Paul was His for as long as He wanted to use him. I realized the entire experience was a reminder that God was in control, and I had to believe He healed my son because He had big plans for Paul's future.

Initially, due to limited oxygen, there was some fear Paul would experience developmental delays. To the contrary, every time we visited the pediatrician, he declared Paul ahead of the milestones for his age. More remarkable, every doctor reminded us that Paul's recovery was a miracle.

Now a freshman in high school, Paul is a starting player on the freshman football team. I was against Paul playing, but I told my husband that the cardiologist would determine whether Paul could play. I assumed Paul's doctor would rule it out. Instead, Dr. Benheim looked me directly in my eyes and asked me a question. "If I had told you that day in the NICU that someday Paul would be able to play football, you would have thought that was great, right?"

Paul has been playing since then. Unlike many children who undergo open-heart surgery, God's healing came with no restrictions.

Have I seen God's hand on my son's life? Yes—from a very young age. The Lord has granted him the gift of compassion. He draws other children to him. When he was just two years old, another mom noticed that her autistic son was always calm when he spent time with Paul during Sunday school. For the next three years, they were placed in the same class. When Paul was planning his fifth birthday party, he said to me, "Mommy, I want to invite Brendan to my party." I thought it was a great idea. He said, "I am going to tell all my friends that Brendan is special, and they need to be nice to him." When I gave the mom the invitation, she cried. She confided in me that no one had ever invited her son to a party, then I cried, too.

There have been countless times through the years where strangers have approached me and shared stories of some kind act that Paul has extended to their child. Every night, I thank God for my miracle baby Paul. I am humbled by the fact that at 14 years old, despite periodic teenage crankiness, he still invites me to pray with him before he goes to sleep each night. I continue to do my job of laying a foundation based on God's word, and I trust that God will reveal the plan he has for Paul's life at the right time.

This is my story, but it is not my life.

ANGELA, FAIRFAX, VA

Like Sarah, I feared I was too old and exhausted to have the baby I wanted. But I believed the promise God made Abraham was for me, too.

In the margin next to Genesis 18: 9-14, I wrote: Baby Lyles, 09/30/94, Then, I prayed.

Oh LORD, if You were able to help Abraham's wife of age 90, I know You can help me make it through my pregnancy at 35. In Jesus Name, Amen.

My husband Richard and I began contemplating having another child when our daughter Kaitlyn begged us for a baby sister, specifically, and began to pray daily for her.

One afternoon, I noticed two phone messages. The first was a sales call I didn't mind missing, but the second one took my breath away. I replayed it over and over. Please God, I can't be hearing this right!

"Valerie," my obstetrician's message said, "your blood shows an extra chromosome 18." Then his empathetic voice changed to a defensive tone.

"Early in the pregnancy, I recommended that you have an amniocentesis just to make sure you didn't need to abort because of your age. This could have been prevented if you had listened to me. Please call the office."

I was jarred from my state of shock when Kaitlyn, home sick from pre-school, walked in, requesting that I refill her empty juice glass.

"More please?"

I walked to the refrigerator, blinking back tears, willing myself to hold it together for Katie Kate and thinking, This cannot be happening. Then I knew I had to turn to turn back to prayer. I could not handle this on my own. *Give me strength, Lord; please give me strength to hold it together for her!*

With Kaitlyn focused on another movie, I escaped upstairs and made the requested return call. Finding that my doctor was out of town for the rest of the week, I spoke with his nurse, who pulled my file. I heard her gasp and say, "I can't tell her this." She gave me no information. She simply said a doctor in the practice would have to call me back.

Four long hours later, another doctor in the practice called and said there was no easy way to share this kind of news. "Your baby has an extra chromosome 18, which means it will die before birth or immediately afterwards. I am sorry."

She recommended that I consider an abortion.

That evening, I spoke often on the phone to Richard and other family members. Later in the evening, I called my friend and neighbor Kathy, who was also pregnant.

Walking the two doors down, I began immediately to share in further detail about my emotional day. She let me talk through my tears for several minutes. But then she put her hands on my shoulders, looked me in the eyes and said, "Get a grip. Now listen, I think your doctor is wrong." Then she asked me a simple question: "How many weeks along were you when that blood test was taken?"

I thought about it. "Twenty-one."

"I am pretty sure that is too late."

After confirming in a medical book that the blood test should be taken between weeks 16 - 18 to ensure accurate results, Kathy continued giving me orders.

"You are leaving that practice and coming over to my doctor's group."

I simply nodded.

The next morning, I called her doctor's group and shared with the receptionist my situation. Placed on hold, I continued praying as I did before calling: *"Please Lord Jesus, I need a miracle, let Kathy's doctor see me!"*

The receptionist said Kathy's doctor was unable to add me to her practice, but another doctor, new to the group, could talk to me that morning.

As I sat across the room from my new obstetrician, I watched him read through my history. Sensing his concern and compassion, I trusted this man.

He looked over his reading glasses and asked: "You had excess amniotic fluid with your first child?"

"Yes."

"Is she ok?"

"Yes, she is perfect!"

"Then my guess is: Lady, you make babies funny. This baby business is not a complete science."

Calling his nurse in, he ordered an ultrasound and amniocentesis.

Waiting by myself for the technician to come begin the tests, I lay on the table, the pros and cons of abortion going through my mind. I had never taken a stance one way or another.

My mother's pastor's wife, a pediatrician, had already asked her: "Valerie can't possibly be thinking about having an abortion, can she?" Her question now influenced my thinking. Was I?

The ultrasound started, and I did not want to watch, until the technician's excited reaction to something made me turn to look. She pointed it out to me: the baby seemed to be waving at us! I saw a tiny little arm and hand waving. It did look like a wave, and I felt like the baby was saying, "Hi Mom, it's me! Hi, Mom, do you see me? I am real, I am alive!"

Tears began streaming down my cheeks, and in a split second, I knew. I knew deep within my heart that I could not destroy this life. This unborn child had every right to live. This baby was alive; and I was not God. It was up to God to decide how long this baby would live.

My new doctor called after two weeks with the long-awaited news. He shared the good news immediately: "Valerie, the baby is fine."

Relief flooded over me. The earlier test result—just as Kathy had suspected—was incorrect due to the time administered.

Kaitlyn's prayers for a baby sister were answered. And on the day I delivered our healthy baby girl in a scheduled C-Section, we announced her name, Sarah.

The baby brought lots of laughter and blessings into our family. None of us could imagine life without her.

Life got into a normal routine, and I was back involved in a weekly Bible study. During the reading of that week's passage my eyes fell upon the opposite page of my Bible where a side note with a date was written in the margin.

Tuning out the discussion, I read, "Baby Lyles" and the verse I'd written alongside: *I will surely return to you about this time next year, and Sarah your wife will have a son.*

A flood of emotions—amazement and disbelief—came over me as I continued to read Genesis, Chapter 18: *Then the LORD said to Abraham, "Why did Sarah laugh and say, 'Will I really have a child, now that I am old?' Is anything too hard for the LORD? I will return to you at the appointed time next year, and Sarah will have a son."*

I checked my watch for the date: September 28, 1995. It was almost one year to the day that I had claimed this verse.

Tears of thankfulness and awe streamed down my face. I felt the Holy Spirit reminding me of what God had done; though I had forgotten my prayer, He had not. He alone had given us Sarah! Blinking back my tears, I wrote a new note next to the first one: Sarah Lyles, 9/28/95.

This is my story, but it is not my life.

VALERIE, ATLANTA, GA

At the age of 29, I was diagnosed with diabetes. The last 35 years, I have been insulin dependent, taking four to five shots daily. While driving home from work in 2001, I placed my left hand over my right eye and found that my vision was blurred. My eye doctor said the tiny blood vessels in my eye were bleeding, caused by many years of out-of-control high blood sugar. The specialist to whom I was referred examined me and explained what was happening and recommended surgery. Then, my eye started to bleed. I had to walk, eat and sleep with my head down for two weeks. After three months, I had another surgery to drain the blood and needed more extensive surgery on the eye, which required me to spend another three weeks with my head held down. All I could do was pray and put medicine in the eye to keep the pressure down. The doctors discovered a hole in my right eye, and nothing could be done for this. I was still putting drops in the eye and traveling back and forth to the doctor. Nothing was helping me, and after a year or two, my vision went dark in that eye. I prayed to the Lord to spare the sight in my left eye. It wasn't until later that I realized that even as I looked at things with my physical sight, I didn't see what God wanted me to see. I was spiritually blind.

My next eye examination didn't turn out well. My doctor told me if I didn't have surgery on my left eye, I was going to lose it, too. I did, and complications set in. My eye started bleeding when I lay down, and a large drop of blood hung over the eye at night. There was so much blood that everything I saw was in black and white. The doctor examined my eye and all he could see was a wall of darkness. I thank God that lasted for only a few days. With bed rest,

I began to see colors again. I still had a long journey ahead of me. I wasn't able to attend church on Sunday mornings with my husband, and I would go to my bedroom and cry.

I came to learn that this was a test of my faith. The good news was God was the instructor, and he wasn't through with me yet.

In June 2010, my eye was bleeding so badly, all I could see was black spots. While lying in the bed, my vision was clear, but when I walked around, it would become cloudy like being in a fog. For three months, I followed light or flashes of white to get around the house. My sight would leave me sporadically, and people didn't understand why I didn't sit down.

I was following the light. A close friend gave me a walking cane to use to find my way around in the house. I was determined to not let it become a crutch for me, so I put it in the kitchen corner. I was being fed, bathed, and cared for by my family, but I was trying to do whatever I could, which is why my vision stayed cloudy. In spite of people visiting and praying for me, I was losing all hope. My flesh was overcoming me.

In July of 2010, my eye was bleeding so badly that I saw thousands of black spots in my view. Every week, I lay in the back seat as my husband drove two hours to the doctor. When the doctor did one surgery to drain the blood out of my eye, there was so much blood that it ran down my face. I thought of Jesus when the crown of thorns was placed on his head, blood running down his face. Still, I gave up.

I told my husband and my uncle that I wasn't going to the doctor that day; I couldn't even get out of the bed. They pleaded with me to see someone who could help me deal with losing my eyesight. I was tired of being led around, tired of going in circles, tired of not being able to go to church. My patience was fading. I was having panic attacks. I couldn't stand to be in a dark room; I had to have the lights on.

The day I decided to go for my eye examination during the last week in August 2010 was a turning point for me. The eye began to improve as I walked around, and my vision wasn't getting cloudy like it had been before. Both my eyes were healing. A great burden had been lifted, and I felt renewed. To God be the glory. As quickly as the problems had started, they seemed to be over. My sight was being restored and my spirit lifted.

It has been five years, and I'm still seeing what God wants me to see. I pray each and every day, and I know, now more than ever, you can have perfect physical sight and still not see what is going on. My brothers and sisters, physical sight is nothing compared to spiritual eyesight. Physical sight shows you to see what is natural in life; spiritual sight opens you up to what God wants you to see.

The Lord wanted me to have spiritual eyesight in, so I could see the things He wanted me to see. Today, I walk by faith not by sight. I'm on that walk of faith in the Lord.

This is my story, but it is not my life.

BERTIE, TISHOMINGO, MS

I am alive on the outside, but I live with a social stigma on the inside. Literally, I carry a virus within my immune system that may activate once every five to seven years, for seven days. I don't know when I contracted it or who shared it with me. I don't even know if I unknowingly have shared it with others.

In the United States, about one out of every six people aged 14 to 49 years have genital herpes. [1]

I left home for college a proud virgin. I was very naïve and quite clueless on sexually transmitted diseases, so as I became sexually active, I was unprepared, and I certainly never thought I would get one. I dated nice, young men from nice families. They appeared to have good hygiene; they were articulate, smart and in college. Even after I graduated from college, I thought my dating selection was fine. I thought there would be some external indication of herpes. I was terribly naïve and playing with fire.

I thought I had a hair bump in a most private area. I couldn't quite see it so I had to get the mirror. I thought it might have been caused by the new soap I was using, but I decided to get it checked out, though I didn't have medical insurance. I visited the health department.

The doctor said it looked consistent with an irritation from soap or bubble bath. I was relieved that she said it did not look like a form of genital herpes. Still, she took a swab for a culture and I left. I never went back for the results because I trusted her assessment. Everything cleared up and life moved on.

---

1   [*Sources: http://www.cdc.gov/std/herpes/stdfact-herpes.htm*]

Five years later, I was in a long-term relationship when I experienced some irritation. I had this sick feeling in my stomach, like I knew the answer to my question. My gynecologist diagnosed me with genital herpes, a diagnosis that was confirmed when I returned to the health department to see the results from my visit five years before.

Around the same time, I found out I was pregnant. Pregnant and unmarried, with genital herpes. I had to tell my boyfriend that I was pregnant and had genital herpes. I had to explain to him about my visit to the health department five years back and what I was told by the physician's assistant. I had such guilt and shame.

How had my life come to this? I'm cultured and educated, with good hygiene. How could I have been so stupid? I wondered if the person who gave this to me knew he was infected. I wondered if I had given it to my boyfriend? My personal stock plummeted. My self-confidence took a major hit and has never recovered.

I married my boyfriend, and we began our family. I was grateful that he would marry me, herpes and all. I didn't feel like the prize I knew I was. Everything else that was shiny and bright about my spirit was compromised by this dormant virus in my immune system. My husband and I had no intimacy, physical or emotional. I was told by more than one marriage counselor that my husband was mentally and emotionally abusive. I allowed that to happen, because I ultimately felt unworthy. I felt he thought he received a booby prize. I can also see that I was mentally and emotionally abusive to myself. My self-talk kept me in place of unworthiness, because I felt no one else would ever want me. And even if they thought they did, I would at some point have to tell them about the virus that lives dormant within my immune system in order to move to another level in the relationship. I had a lot of healing to do in my spirit, and I had to forgive myself for my ignorance. But I had nowhere to go for support with this subject. It is a stigma; there is no support or survivor's group for the life sentence of this virus. You won't receive empathy, and you won't want any because you don't want anyone to know. It took me almost 20 years to have the courage to leave a toxic marriage and decide I am worthy of a relationship that wasn't emotionally abusive and void relationship.

I have a friend who courageously shares that she has genital herpes. She dates and shares that some of the men she meets just can't deal with the existence of the virus. The only reason I know she has it is, because other people have shared it with me in mixed company. Although she may be candid with her situation, I choose not to be so free with my dilemma. The last thing I want is for this to be discussed with others. I write this with anonymity.

This is the first step toward healing, freeing myself from the fear of personal rejection and forgiving myself. Only God could give me the courage to give this testimony and use it to help others heal, too.

It is my prayer that a dialogue between women can come from my testimony and that support for people living and dating with genital herpes and other incurable STDs will increase.

I pray that there will be understanding and, ultimately, dignity.

This is my story, but it is not my life.

GRACE, CHARLOTTE, NC

I sat on an exam table, in my underwear, nervously swinging my skinny legs, thinking, Why are doctor's offices so cold? I was 9, and I wanted to be out playing like other kids. While I waited, I chewed, absentmindedly on my long, front braid and fiddled with the ribbons holding the other two.

When the door opened, I thought it was my regular doctor and my parents. I was wrong.

A doctor I had never seen walked in, with a line of white-coated interns in tow. I froze, feeling unfamiliar eyes on my spots.

Please go away, I thought.

The doctor didn't talk to me or acknowledge me in any way. He did, however, grab my arm, holding it up for the interns to inspect. "This is vitiligo," he said.

As though I was no more than the spots on my skin, he explained there was no cure for my ailment. There is a sudden pain in my stomach.

I stared at the floor, stunned, mentally removing myself from the room "At least," he continued, "she can cover up most of her body." He sounded a million miles away.

He positioned my arm so the doctors-in-training could see it fully. "Unfortunately, she can't do anything about her hands and face." Then, done with his lesson, he released my arm and exited.

I was 7 when a little spot appeared on my forehead. I don't remember ever wondering what it was; I was too busy being a child. That little spot grew, covering my face and neck. New spots appeared on my legs and arms. My vitiligo spread rapidly, confounding doctors and distressing my parents. Still, I don't remember being aware of what was happening to me. I do remember that everyone else seemed to be all too aware of it. Their voices stayed in my head. Some were just curious. "Did you get burned?" "Does it hurt?" Most were less than kind.

"Can I catch it from you?" "You look like a corpse." "How can you stand having that all over you?"

I wanted to disappear. So I practiced being small, insignificant, separate. If I could go unnoticed, no one would hurt me. In my mind, being ignored was far better than being bullied. No matter how invisible I tried to be, pain always found me. I couldn't hide from it. My parents loved and supported me, but they couldn't fix me. I knew about God, but I didn't know God, and I certainly didn't think He knew me. My Catholic upbringing made Him a familiar figure but not an accessible one. I was more familiar with guilt and disappointment than hope. I knew a lot about duty but nothing about grace. The funny thing was, I felt I knew enough to question Him.

Why do I look like this?

When I was 13, my family moved out of the neighborhood where we had lived since the summer I turned 4. In my old neighborhood, I knew where my safe zones were, which teachers would look out for me and which kids to avoid. All that changed. Being the new kid was hard. Being the new, spotted kid with the heavy makeup was terrifying. Soon, everybody knew about me. I was overwhelmed. So I boxed up my feelings and packed them away. Allowing myself to be vulnerable was not an option. I didn't cry or retaliate or complain when the attacks came. Afraid the pain would overtake me, I took every pointed word and stuffed it in my box until I couldn't feel it anymore. Unfortunately, I could not hide from my own voice. Why am I so ugly?

With my feelings neatly packed away, I got really good at pretending my condition didn't bother me. By the time I entered high school, I had gone from wishing to be normal to accepting what was. I was determined to make vitiligo a non-issue in my life. No more visits to dermatologists. No more pills, lotions or potions. No more hoping for a cure. Unhindered by my boxed-up emotions, my confidence grew. I went from avoiding everything in middle school to joining everything in high school, deciding that if people were going to stare at me, they were going to do it on my terms. I became obsessed with fashion. I threw myself into performing arts and public speaking. To my surprise, I had more friends and fewer people I had to avoid. Staying chronically busy left me no time to deal with my stuff. Even my family and closest friends didn't know how scared and insecure I really was. I would never have sincerely talked to anyone about my disease. When people asked about it, I offered mature, practiced statements that made it all seem like no big deal. I almost believed what I was saying.

In college, I started studying the Bible. Eventually, I accepted Christ and began to get to know God. Though I grew and changed more than I ever could have imagined, I overlooked my pain. Finding God did not free me from my past, because I wouldn't trust Him with it. Long after I professed my faith, my insecurities still controlled me. The truth was, I believed the insults I had been hearing my whole life. My mother always told me I was beautiful, but I owned the names other people called me. I had loyal friends around me, but I could still see the faces of kids who were scared I was contagious. My husband and kids adored me, but secretly, I didn't believe I was worthy of being loved or respected. I never admitted that to anyone. I would not unpack that box. And I never, ever prayed about my pain.

Why do I have to be like this?

Recently, a deacon at my church told me that his new grandbaby had vitiligo. My heart sank. I was so sorry. I knew she would be bullied by other kids. I knew that her self-esteem would be battered. I wondered if she would ever feel beautiful or, at least, normal. I gathered myself, preparing to suggest doctors and list treatment options.

"Have they taken her to a dermatologist?" I asked.

"My daughter is upset and doesn't want to talk about it. But I told her not to worry because her baby girl was going to grow up to be like you."

Me? I didn't know what to say.

"Every time I see you, I know she is going to be fine. Pretty and confident, just like you."

I heard God say, "That's why I made you the way you are."

I felt like I could draw a line from my pain directly to that moment. Despite my past (or maybe because of it), my illness was a blessing to someone I barely knew! My vitiligo gave Deacon the hope that I wouldn't allow myself to have. If I could commit to pray about his granddaughter's future, why couldn't I decide to pray to release my past? I can give many examples of how God used my illness to shape me and help the people I love. But few things have ever helped me see God's plan so clearly.

It is a miracle when someone sees something in you that you don't see; something that has grown out of the trials God uses for His purposes and our good. I am still learning to value myself. I don't see what Deacon sees. My vitiligo is spreading again. I battle with the mirror every morning, analyzing my new spots and obsessing over my makeup. I wear long pants in the dead of summer and I still notice when the cashier at Kroger tries to take my money without touching my hand.

But God is still at work in my life. Instead of pretending my vitiligo is not an issue, I pray daily for healing. I believe that I will be healed, inside and out. But, I am also sure that if it is not His plan to heal me on this side of Heaven, His grace is, indeed, sufficient. I still don't see myself as my parents see me, as my husband sees me, as my God sees me, but I am working on it.

This is my story, but it is not my life.

KAREN, DECATUR, GA

My heart disease affected me and my family, and eventually, I had to have a heart transplant. God made it possible, and I received a miracle in the form of a brand new heart on Thursday, May 3, 2012. Eight weeks after receiving my new heart, I was on the neighborhood track walking, with my youngest son cheering me on. I had not been able to exercise without stopping and gasping for air for at least 18 months. I was ecstatic to have a basic conversation, eat and even laugh—all of which had been extremely difficult for me before the transplant.

Now, almost four years later, I am on the road to living life again, I'm mothering my kids, being a great wife, daughter, soror and friend, and I'm even returning to work as a teacher. I was truly given a second chance to live!

Heart disease began to affect my life and that of my family and friends in 2002; when I was 37 years old. Diagnosed with dilated cardiomyopathy, I had to stop teaching for periods at a time between 2002 and 2011, sometimes taking leave without pay. My husband did not complain. He joyfully took care of our 2-year-old son and took me to my appointments with cardiologists. My parents, my husband's mother, our extended family and friends also supported us whenever we needed their support.

Initially, a cocktail of medications maintained my heart function, and I felt fine. The medicines controlled hypertension, heart function and prevented blood clots. I religiously went to the gym, participated in step and spinning classes, as well as walking and bike riding. In 2004, I trained and walked 30 of 39 miles in the Susan G. Komen Breast Cancer 2-Day Walk in honor of my mother-in-law.

In 2005, I believe my God sent my (now) oldest son to save my life during a cardiac incident. When he climbed into our bed in the middle of the night, he woke me up. Irritated by his presence at that late hour, I rolled over and experienced a funny feeling in my chest. I was cold and clammy and passed out. My husband called the paramedics. Once in the hospital, I learned I had suffered a heart attack!

My issues were beginning again. The heart attack meant more problems for my family to contend with and more time off of work. My cardiologists encouraged me to get an implanted bi-ventricular pacemaker. This device is a combination pacemaker and defibrillator used to synchronize the contractions of the left ventricle with the right ventricle and to improve heart function in patients with severe and moderately severe symptoms of heart failure. I knew it was necessary, but I was equally frightened by the thought of surgery and the thought of having a visible scar and a huge lump protruding just above my left breast.

I acquiesced when I learned that one of the characteristics of this disease is sudden death due to the heart stopping. Once I healed from implantation surgery, I joined a fit boot camp to continue exercising and staying in shape; the trainer modified the exercises for me because of my heart. Walking daily was also a part of my heart healthy routine. My family and I also ate healthily and created a Biggest Loser family version so they, too, could eat well and protect their hearts.

In 2008, I passed out in front of my students. It was scary for the students and me. Fortunately, I had the bi-ventricular pacemaker. Doctors said that without it, I would have died. I passed out three additional times, and each time, the electrophysiologists said that I was saved from death by my device. The second time I passed out, I was home with my oldest son. He was scared and said that I appeared comatose. He did not know what to do, but the device revived me within a matter of seconds!

I could not drive for three months after each episode. This put a strain on our family because my husband or my parents had to take me everywhere I needed to go. Although they never complained, I felt like such a burden.

There were other highs and lows between 2008 and 2011.

In 2010 my husband and oldest son flew to Ethiopia to complete the adoption of our youngest son. I could not go with them because, weeks before the trip, my cardiologist nixed travel. He believed my heart was too weak and feared I might have a fainting episode that Ethiopian doctors could not have handled. My Ethiopian son has never seen me healthy. He did not understand why some days I was in bed when he left for school and when he returned from school. My oldest son shared the fun we used to have before my heart got sick.

I could no longer handle teaching five classes of 25+ kids so, in the 2010-2011 school year, my principal named me the in-school suspension coordinator where I had, at most, 10 students a day. Some days, I did not have any students and was able to sit still; not placing any stress on my heart.

In September 2011, my heart health deteriorated to a point where I stopped working, and my doctor began evaluating me for the heart transplant list. I lay in bed for days at a time, gave up driving, did not want to go out, could not walk up and down steps and depended on everyone to bring me what I needed. My physical appearance changed. I lost weight because the blood and oxygen were not flowing through my body. I lost my appetite, and my complexion went from chocolate brown to a pale-ashy browning gray. I felt bad, and I knew that a heart transplant was the answer. The thought was never scary to me, because I knew God would protect me and my family. I was blessed to be placed on the heart transplant list in December 2011.

In April 2012, my cardiologist admitted me to the cardiac intensive care unit (ICU) to await a new heart. Doctors and nurses predicted the wait for a new heart could range from a week to 12 months or even longer. I am blessed and highly favored; my wait was only 21 days. During my time in the hospital, I grew closer to God, because all I could do was pray. One of the conditions of being in ICU was complete bed rest and having a painful swan catheter enter my neck and travel to my heart. The catheter remained in my neck until my heart transplant, and additional injections and tubes caused me to call on Jesus several times, especially at night.

It was miserable. Still, God sent His angels to help comfort me while I was in ICU. One night, I cried and cried and considered leaving ICU to wait at home for my transplant, though doing so would have placed me lower on the list. Nurse Ivy sang to me whenever I cried. And a maintenance engineer, Ray, came in and began a conversation. He told me that I was in his room. I was not in the mood to talk, but I felt obligated to talk to him and asked what he meant. It was his room 10 years before when he was awaiting a transplant. He joined the hospital staff after his transplant and also became a spokesperson for transplant patients. God sent Ray to comfort me. Ray visited me every night and shared words of encouragement. Today, Ray is still in touch with my family and me. His friendship and his experiences helped make waiting easier.

While I was in the hospital, I video-conferenced my kids and other family members and enjoyed watching my husband become Mr. Mom. Every day during my 33-day stay in the hospital, someone from my family drove 25 miles each way to visit me, so I would never feel lonely. I did not get to see my kids much during my hospital stay, and I missed them tremendously. My husband even turned my hospital room into his office and worked from my hospital room. He even spent a few nights with me.

My Delta Sigma Theta sorors organized a prayer visit and Skype teleconference from my hospital room. Soror Minister Susan prayed so hard and strong for me, I felt like I could've walked out of ICU that very moment. God was working on my behalf.

May 3, 2012, was a day indeed. My husband spent the night in the hospital with me because I was traumatized by a failed procedure the night before. One of my girlfriends brought a few sugary treats for me, and for lunch, I ordered shrimp scampi, coconut shrimp and cheesecake. My lunch was delayed by hours, and I was starving. Nurses kept coming into my room giving me conflicting instructions. Eat your lunch. Don't eat or drink anything. I was hungry and very angry.

Then, a very chipper orderly came in and let it slip that a heart had been located. A cardiologist flew to assess it and, possibly, bring it back for me.

What? God, please let the heart be a match. God, please comfort the family of my donor, because I know they are probably in mourning right now.

One by one, my cardiac team trickled into my small room, smiling cautiously optimistic smiles. I signed what felt like millions of papers. It was approximately 2:30 p.m., and the operating room was reserved for 4:00 p.m. The closer it got to the surgery, the more optimistic they seemed. They gave me something to relax, and less than 24 hours later, I awoke, the breathing tube was removed and my new life began. The nurses told me I was going to walk with their assistance. I required lots of assistance but walked 10 feet and sat in a chair.

Between May 4, 2012, and May 18, 2012, my endurance increased, and I was able to walk two miles on my own—required by my surgeon for my release. The nurses were super-impressed by my progress and said they'd never seen a transplant patient progress the way I did. God did that for me.

Once I was released from the hospital, I took nearly a hundred pills and tablets daily. I attended 36 sessions of cardiac rehabilitation and, over time, was able to complete 25 to 30 minutes of uninterrupted activity in the cardiac rehabilitation gym each visit. I joined a boot camp, resumed walking regularly, rode bikes with my sons, took cruise vacations with my family and began to enjoy life again. Today, three and a half years later, I am pleased to report that my new heart and I are doing wonderfully well. Heart transplant patients are required to have periodic biopsies to check for rejection, and we hope for a score of zero. I've received more than 20 zeros and I am grateful.

A donor saved my life. You could do the same for someone, too.

This is my story, but it is not my life.

JOY, NASSAU, BAHAMAS

MOTHERS

Psalm 27:10 Even if my father and mother abandon me, the Lord will hold me close. (NLT)

I was 3 years old the first time I was broken. My mother was arrested for the first of many times, and I saw the whole thing. I remember going to my aunt's house and asking her where my mom was. She simply hugged me and said we had to pray for my mother. Then, she put me to bed with my cousins.

This would become a way of life for us. My mom would do something, be arrested, and I would go live with my aunt. The cycle didn't break until I was 8. While visiting my aunt for the summer, I told her about my mom's new boyfriend and how he had once asked me to lie on his chest while he rubbed my back. My aunt called my mom and simply told her I was not coming back. To my knowledge, my mother never questioned her sister. She simply gave me to my aunt.

After living quite happily with my aunt for a year or so, this brilliant, beautiful angel—who had always come to my rescue and defense and made me feel wanted and loved—had a sudden massive stroke and died. Life as I had come to know it ended. I spent the remainder of my childhood with another aunt.

I have never known why my own mother never came to get me. I talked to her by phone and visited once in a while, but I felt responsible for her absence. She took my younger brother by a different father, so I assumed I was too bad of a child for anyone to love.

Sometimes, I feel like a motherless daughter, even though my mom is still alive. I miss the mom I never knew.

I have lots of happy memories of growing up in my family. What stands out most, though, are the memories I don't have: being hugged and kissed, being listened to, being complimented. I began to believe that I had to earn those things, so I worked harder and harder to get the love I so desperately craved. I always got good grades. I tried to be fiercely independent even at a young age. I tried to be perfect. I built an incredible wall around myself and spent the last 35 years of my life trying to earn my mother's approval, pride and love. I participated in extra-curricular activities, had a part-time job, earned awards and was the first person in my immediate family to earn a scholarship to college. But it wasn't enough to earn her approval.

I married my high school sweetheart after college, had two beautiful children, bought a home, traveled the country and paid for her to join us. It still wasn't enough. When I needed her, when I had the courage to face my fear of rejection and ask her for her presence, she chose her own needs or the needs of one of my siblings. Today, the cycle continues: She rejects me, I feel hurt and angry, I feel guilty for feeling angry, and we pretend everything is okay until she rejects me again.

Fortunately, I've come to have faith in God's plan for me. God is helping me heal, and I am beginning to understand and accept the tragedy of my relationship with Mom and why she remains emotionally unavailable to me. Still, understanding it doesn't take away the damage that was done.

It is rare that we discuss motherless women or the unique and tremendously hurtful issue of abandonment they face. My anticipation of my daughter's arrival stirred up a different and unfamiliar batch of emotions. My excitement was through the roof and even though I had been mothering my son in a way I thought was exceptional, I felt somewhat inadequate.

I thought, "This is the girl I've waited so long for. How will I know what to do, and if I'm doing it right?" But more scary for me was the bigger question: "How can I love her the way she needs when I don't know what it feels like to be loved by my mother?"

I still don't have answers. But I pray constantly asking God in his divine artistry to guide me. Figuring it out is part of my journey. What I do know so far is that my children are amazing, truly one of my biggest blessings. What I feel is an unbreakable bond. They know they can count on me both to praise and, when necessary, to scold.

My life experiences helped to shape me into the woman I am. Without them, maybe I wouldn't have come to rely on my faith. Maybe I wouldn't have ended up with a loving, supportive husband, who is my best friend, and the two smart and sassy children we adore. I wouldn't change how things have turned out. You see, I took those pieces that I thought were broken and useless, and I gave them to God. And He took what I thought was worthless and unlovable and arranged all the pieces into this beautiful thing I call my life.

From a little girl who felt abandoned, came a woman with a family of her own—one who counts on her. I know I am needed and more importantly, wanted and loved. Statistics say I should not have the life I have. But GOD saw a beauty in the broken pieces, he saw in me what I and others could not see. God took my life and made it a work of art... I am God's Mosaic.

This is my story, but it is not my life.

ROSE, MEMPHIS, TN

The hospital doors opened, and I was running. My black boots hit the cold tile floors, one foot after the other, as fast as I could move them, my cape hitting the back of my calves as I ran, my red scarf flying about my face. Many details I have forgotten about that cold December day, but I remember the red scarf, its color so bright against the muted colors in that long hallway. I don't know why I remember that red scarf so vividly, but I do. That red scarf…my symbol of the day my busy life lost control, the day my well-planned world turned upside down, the last day my beloved mom and I would ever laugh together. My heart shattered in a million pieces; it was the beginning of a hellish journey I could never have imagined. My red scarf…a lasting symbol that I survived tragedy, even though I often believed I could not bear one more second of the searing pain.

The phone at my house had rung. When I picked up, Dad said, "I need you to come to the hospital, but I need you to be safe."

"What?" I asked him three times, trying to make sense of what he was saying. Then, he uttered the words that made my heart skip a beat. "Your momma stopped breathing. They are working on her, but it looks bad. I need you to come to the hospital, but I need you to be safe."

I barely heard the rest of his words. I do not even recall exactly what I said, other than to let him know I was on my way. I stopped to pray with my mother-in-law, and I continued to pray and bargain with God on the drive to the hospital. "Anything, God, anything… Please, just don't let her die, please don't let her die."

I drove like a bat out of hell. Later, my dad would say, that I arrived "Fast... scary fast." I have no idea how long it took me to get there, but the next thing I know, I was running down that hall, with my red scarf flying about me, heading to the elevators which would take me to the floor where my mom's room was.

I remember the looks on people's faces as I ran. Curious. Puzzled. Irritated. Bewildered. I recall wondering why they looked at me so strangely. I also recall how everything seemed to move so slowly, as if everyone was moving in slow-motion, strangers parting down the middle of the hallway to let me pass. I know I wasn't moving slowly, but the images replay in my mind in slow motion and with practically no color...except that red scarf.

It turns out, the hell that awaited me upstairs was nothing I could have ever imagined, and maybe my mind slows down that run down the hall on purpose, so I could hang onto life as I knew it for a few moments longer.

My mother did not die that day, at least not technically. She stopped breathing, and they resuscitated her. They got her back. But the truth is, we did not. The laughing, loving mother, adoring wife, doting grandmother, cherished sister, aunt, cousin, and friend was gone.

Our minds revolt against calling a person a vegetable. And until you have seen someone in a persistent vegetative state or minimally conscious existence, you cannot begin to recognize the catastrophic destruction that a severe anoxic brain injury is. It robs a person of what makes that person who they are.

There is no way I can describe the horror of the next year. My once brilliant, graceful, and beautiful mother often screamed, thrashed, bit, kicked and threw her body, legs and arms so viciously that, once, she almost broke her own nose. She would alternately sit and stare into nothingness or scream for hours at a time in a painfully woeful pitch... so loud you could hear her from the doors of the facility when you walked in, even though her room was at the back of the facility....making sounds my mother never would have made before this awful event occurred. She could not walk, sit up or control any bodily functions. Once, she bit my finger so hard, the nail grew out with a hole in it that took months to go away. Her immune system was depleted also. She developed thrush in her mouth repeatedly as well as other infections during the following year.

We sat by her side—watching, praying, crying, singing, consulting doctors, trying everything. We sat watching my father's tremendous pain as he watched the tortured body of his beloved—all as we tried to find a way to adjust to this strange new life, tending to her incredible medical needs, dealing with our own grief and pain, as well as each other's, and all the while praying and holding out hope for a miracle.

And oh, how I prayed. At first, I prayed with absolute faith that she would be healed and be our very own Christmas miracle. My parents were truly good, Christian people. They didn't cheat, lie or steal, and they worked so hard their entire lives, sacrificing so much to make life better for my brother and me. Throughout their marriage, they had taken in so many people, I had lost count, and they helped support grandparents, parents, siblings, cousins, nephews, nieces, and even total strangers.

My mother didn't drink or curse. She had faith…of course she would be healed. God was good, God was fair, and so many good people were praying hard for her across the country, around the clock. Of course, God would heal her.

As the weeks stretched into months and the pain intensified, doctors' predictions grew more grim, facilities complained about her presence and expenses mounted. Still, I prayed …but with more desperation: Please God, please. We can't take it anymore. Show us some sign. Take this pain away. Take me away. Anything. Please.

I wish I could say my faith remained strong, and I trusted God in His wisdom the entire time, but after months of facing the devastation of what was left of my beautiful mother, her screaming, thrashing body—and witnessing weeks of watching my father, heartbroken, by her side, my entire family and me tortured—I began to question God: How could you allow this? Why don't you fix this? Why does anyone have to live like this? Why have you put me here through this when I can do nothing? What is the purpose of this pain? Why? Why? Why?

The months and the pain continued. My faith wavered, and I grew afraid to pray. After all, I had prayed for her not to die, and look what happened. I begged silently, God, please open up the ground and swallow me in the hole. I don't want to be here anymore. I can't stand to see her cry and scream anymore. I can't watch my father's heart break one more second. I can't bear my children's tears anymore, my brother's pain, my uncles' anguish. This loss… this powerlessness… this senseless waste of her precious, beautiful life. Why, God, why?

My mother's body finally gave out almost a year to the day after the code. She is at peace now, and I know she sings with the angels. I wish I could say her death was easy, but even though it was a blessing to end her suffering, it meant she was truly gone from us. The loss was tremendous. The weight of the prior year hit hard and was a heavy burden to carry. I wish I could say my walk back to faith happened in one easy step or one big event, but it did not. The pain and fear of that year left us in pieces, and the walk back was in baby steps.

I came to realize, however, that, God had not abandoned us that year. He had been there the whole time, holding us through the arms of His people. Our church family and friends had steadfastly been there for us that whole time, loving us, supporting us, and praying for us, even when we could not pray for ourselves. We had help with everyday chores and caring for Mom, taking shifts at the hospital, reading to her and praying over her. And the help always was offered with grace, smiles, hugs, and love. It reminded us of His Grace. He was there in His people. He was there when I found the strength to pick myself up off the floor where I lay broken and crying. He was there when my arms comforted my children and when my husband held me as I sobbed at night. He was there when I listened to my Dad break down because Mom cried as he left her room. He was there.

I do not know why God heals some people and does not heal others. I may never have a good answer as to why my mother had to endure what she did, but I do know God was there, and I know I survived it. I know my faith came back, even if it took the long way home. I know now there are things worse than death, and I know I have lived through one of them. I know I do not wish to do so again, but I know God would be there if I had to do so. I also know that, for whatever reason, I still have that red scarf and I love it. It reminds me of what I lost, but it also reminds me I survived. I wear it with pride.

This is my story, but it is not my life.

TERESA P., ATLANTA, GA

"Hello?"

"Connie, Mom had a stroke; it's not good. You have to get here, fast!"

I will never forget that phone call from my sister for as long as I live. It was the beginning of one of the worst days of my life.

My husband, our four children and I were attending a Bible college in rural Indiana, and we were beginning year two of our two-year in-residence training program to become ministers. We spent hours each day reading and studying God's Word, preparing for a life of Christian service. You would think that my heart would be prepared for something like this, but nothing could have prepared me for that call.

Interestingly enough, the night before this occurred, I was in a meeting with a speaker who was a wise elderly woman with a wonderful heart for God. As she shared God's Word, she said something that I know was just for me. Sometimes in life, she reminded me, things happen that we don't understand, but we have to rest assured that God is always with us to comfort us and to strengthen us. That is something we must never forget, no matter what. She and I spoke a few weeks later, and she told me that wasn't what she had planned to share, but God put that on her heart.

After I hung up the phone, I quickly found my husband and told him the horrible news, and we prepared to make the long journey from Indiana to Utah to say goodbye to my mother – the woman who gave birth to me, the woman I struggled to understand, the woman that I was often too hard on; the most important person in my life. I wish I could have had one more conversation, one more visit, with her.

Three weeks earlier, we spent two weeks in Utah before heading back to Indiana. It was a pleasant trip, but with four children under the age of 8, I was always planning for the next thing and did not often take time to enjoy the moment. One evening, my mother wanted to do a sleep over with all of her grandchildren. I wasn't invited, because she said I would try to ruin the fun. She may have been right. Her plan was to let them stay up as long as they wanted and indulge in root beer floats, movies and other fun activities.

She was fun, and everybody loved her. She was undoubtedly the life of every party. For as long as I could remember, everyone just wanted to be around her. She had the voice of an angel that I never appreciated until she was gone. She could connect to anyone anywhere, and no one was a stranger in her home. Though her youngest daughter, I did not share her free-spirited nature. I was not very fun or affectionate, and she struggled to connect with me, but it didn't stop her from trying.

I had very firm ideas about who I wanted her to be. I wanted a mom who put cooked meals on the table, who kept the house spotless, who paid the bills on time, who was more responsible, at least from my perspective. What I got, instead, was someone who sometimes cooked and sometimes didn't, which resulted in me learning to cook myself. My mom was someone who couldn't care less how the house looked, but would sit down and have an intimate conversation with whomever needed it; someone who occasionally didn't pay the bills on time resulting in no electricity for a brief time; someone who was striving to live her life the best she could. She tried so hard.

My parents divorced when I was 7 and in my eyes, when my dad left, so did my stability. He and I were very similar, and I learned to take life a bit too seriously as a child. I never learned how to have fun, because I equated fun with irresponsibility. What I failed to realize about my mother was that she was a person too. She was a single mother of four children. At times, she worked two jobs to make ends meet, and sometimes they still didn't meet. I didn't cut her any slack. Only after becoming a mother myself did I begin to have compassion for her. I realized that there is no manual on motherhood; you do the best you can with what you have. It's a hard and thankless job at times, but one I wouldn't trade for anything. It is truly a privilege to be allowed to mother human beings, to guide and nurture them. I didn't realize it, but my mother taught me so many valuable lessons, as she continued to learn herself.

During my somewhat tumultuous childhood, I always had a desire to know God, but I never really knew how to get to Him. I went to church occasionally, but that didn't help me. In fact, I often left church more confused about who God was and what He meant to me. I did however; know that I wanted to know Him. I knew He was important to know and that a relationship with Him would help me, but I just didn't know how to get to Him.

In the spring of 1983 as a freshmen in college, my soon-to-be husband introduced me to a class, Power for Abundant Living. It was a class that taught me how to read and understand the Bible, which in turn taught me how to live life with God. I learned that God is a God of love – not this being that was waiting to cause me difficulty or teach me a lesson, but a loving Heavenly Father who was always there for me. I learned that His Word was His will and if I wanted to know Him, I needed to know His Word. It was fantastic to finally know and develop an intimate relationship with this God I had longed to know.

However, even with my newly developing relationship with God, I still had a hard heart toward my mom. Actually, I had a hard heart in general. Over the years, I realized my need to control anything and everything that I was up against. I feared I would not be okay and thought I could avoid difficulties in my life if I could get everyone to behave the way that I wanted them to. That wasn't the case. In fact, the more I tried to control, the more I lost control; it was a vicious cycle.

On September 17, 1995, I made my way home to say goodbye to my mother. She had hung on, but once all of her children arrived, they took her off of life support. I held her hand, I prayed for her, and I told her how much I loved her. They told us it would be an hour or so before she was gone. But as had always been the case, she lived on her own terms. She hung on for many more hours, then she went to sleep for good.

The next few days were a bit of a daze for me. But the pain in my heart was like no other. I needed to figure out a way to control the pain or, I thought, it would ruin me. I tried and tried to figure it out myself, to no avail, so I finally turned to God. I poured my heart out to Him and asked Him to help me; it was too hard for me alone.

As He always does, God answered my cry. As the days went on, there was still pain in my heart, but it lessened. I had hope that I would one day be able to think of her without the tears and the pain.

Now 20 years later, I am so thankful for my mother. The tears and pain have ended, but there will always be a void where my mother's presence once was. I am so thankful for what she taught me. She taught me strength and compassion; love and passion. I only wish that I had the chance to tell her how much she meant to me, to tell her how beautiful she was and that I understand how hard it was for her.

As a mother of adult children, I often reflect on how we receive no training for motherhood. Our parenting mimics our experience. My mom had no manual; she just endeavored to love us and care for us the best she could. She didn't always do it right and neither do I, but I know beyond a shadow of a doubt that she loved us and only wanted the best for us. Today, I understand that my mom wasn't perfect, but her heart was in the right place, and she did the very best she could. I couldn't have asked for a better role model.

This is my story, but it's not my life.

CONNIE, SALT LAKE CITY, UT

As a young girl growing up in California, I believed my mother was invincible. Mom was a single mother. She always worked. And I thought she could do anything, anything she set her mind to.

After my father and my mother divorced, Aunt Pearl, a friend who often was my babysitter, asked my mom if she could adopt me. Though Aunt Pearl kept me every day, she did not adopt me.

Something about watching my mother working so hard taught me a strong work ethic and shaped my character. In many ways, we became one. I see myself in her. There are a lot of things, however, I try not to see – for instance, the time my mother took my aunt's inheritance from under her. She had my aunt sign paperwork for a house they owned jointly. The papers were then stored away for more than two decades. Then when I was a teenager, my mom pulled out the paperwork, took it to court and obtained sole ownership of the house. I never understood how my mother could do this to my aunt, her only sister.

I learned about it just after college. My mother tried to justify her actions by saying she was doing it for the well-being of all the family. But why did she do it with such secrecy? Finding this out changed me. Moreso, it changed the way I think of my mother to this day.

I grew up never thinking about becoming a wife and mother, but becoming a mother was a gift. Motherhood taught me selflessness. Everything I do is for my children, so choosing to leave my job and the possibility of a career was a natural decision.

I actually became the opposite of my mother. I am married; she was single. I have been able to stay home; she worked. My husband is my partner; my father never helped with anything except to conceive me. In many ways, I believe watching me as mom has caused my mother pain, while I hoped it would give her joy. But I guess there are a lot of things I will never fully understand.

My grandmother never worked and never stepped fully into motherhood, so my mother had to grow up fast to care for her younger siblings. By age nine, she was Mom to her brothers and sister. Now, I sense that she is tired from working so hard and struggling so long.

Maybe because she has taken care of others for so long my mother has chosen not to be more involved. It is, perhaps, because of raising children at such an early age that she is not a traditional grandmother to her grandchildren. I can count the number of times on one hand that she has spent one-on-one time with her grandchildren.

We aren't what you would call close. I think she wants us to be, but she stays busy so she doesn't have to confront her truths. She pretends to be okay, but pain has a way of sticking around. We are so far apart in our station in life that coming together is difficult. Even though she is over 70 years old, she is still focused on achieving some greater level of success in her life. Every decision, every action – all of her energy – is focused on her work. She begins her sentences with work and ends her sentences with work. Work is her oxygen. It is hard to reach her on a spirit level because she is hiding behind her demons. I had a decision to make when it comes to loving my mother. That decision involved how best to love her given where she is in her life and where I am in mine. My objective has always been to understand and to find a way to love her unconditionally. My faith has enabled me to begin that journey.

After I returned home from college, my mother and I went from being two peas in a pod to being distanced. I began to pray for understanding, and as I've grown stronger in my faith, I have asked God for strength to see her goodness. I need God to reveal to her all those things in her that caused me to question my true love for her. I know that we all have our faults; I do not try to judge her. I pray daily for the ability to love my mom without restrictions.

One of my biggest regrets is my inability to talk to my mother openly and truthfully. I don't want to hurt her, but I want us to be closer. It is hard for me to love her when there are so many things I have not been able to forgive. I am trying. I am praying for that ability to forgive. It is what God wants and expects of me.

If I had that opportunity to sit down with her and have a fully transparent conversation, I would tell her that I want to forgive her even if she does not think there is anything she has done wrong. I would tell her I am forgiving her for deceiving my aunt. I would tell her I want to forgive her for not hugging me more. I want to forgive her for my feeling incompletely loved as a child. I want to forgive her for taking shortcuts when it comes to managing the affairs of her life. But most important, I really want to forgive her for not fixing between us what I know she sees, what she too feels, is broken.

So I pray, and I pray, and I pray. I trust God to show me His will in my life. I know that there is something to be learned in this life's journey. I was created to walk out my life and that is what I am trying to do with excellence. I know that this journey must include fixing some things with my mother while there is still time.

Recently, my phone rang. The caller ID showed Mom. I was actually relieved. I was grateful to know that I have time with her on earth and that there is still time in the flesh to work out the distance between us.

I love my mother, and I know she loves me. Through Christ, I can better appreciate the struggles she has been through. While I do not blame her entirely for the weaknesses in our relationship, I pray continuously that the rest of the time we have together will be better.

Sometimes I hear myself yelling, "Stop, Mom! Let's just stop now and be real with each another. I am your daughter, and I want to know that we have something lasting and real between us. I don't want to live in the past. I want to create memories in the now based on truth and transparency. I want to know that we can be who we are with each another and accept each other exactly as we are. I want to hear you say, 'I love you. I am proud of you. I cherish your involvement in my life'."

I believe we can get there. In Christ's name, I claim it to be so.

This is my story, but it is not my life.

ME, LOS ANGELES, CA

It takes a lot of courage to say this: I did not like my mother. I loved her more than anything. In fact, on the love scale, what I felt for my mother was probably closer to worship. But I am not sure I really liked her much.

My mother was beautiful physically. Her skin smooth as silk. She was a mocha vision of perfection. She dressed immaculately. She smelled like lavender. Her hair shined like diamonds. She smiled in a way that drew others in. She was, in her own way, an African princess. Yet, in spite of all her attributes, she was a colossal mess. And I resented her for it. I spent most of my childhood and the early part of my adulthood trying to erase how much I did not like her behavior and running from how much I loved her. The stain on our relationship was her depression and her alcoholism. As an 8-year-old watching her mother destroy her life one drink at a time, it was difficult to separate the knowledge of her sickness from having to go into the world and pretend everything was perfect when nothing could have been further from the truth.

Babysitting my mother during my childhood took its toll on me. After she and my father divorced, I never knew which boyfriend – at my mother's insistence, we called them, "uncle" – was going to bring her home. She didn't overlap men; in fact, she had long, though not enduring, intimate relationships. One night, Uncle Bill brought her home. Uncle Bill was white and wore expensive red cowboy boots. And since I couldn't find a white person named Bill anywhere on our Mississippi family tree, I went out of my way to run him off. It took about four weeks. My siblings and I were just horrible to him. In retrospect, I feel kind of bad about the way we treated Mr. Bill. Mr. Bill was a nice guy whose only infraction was showing up too late and too far down on the list of uncles.

On at least one occasion, Momma came home bruised and battered. After that, waiting up, sitting up, to see just how she would make it home became a job we completed in shifts. My oldest brother used to always say, "I'll take it from here. I'll wake you if I need you." We never slept, unless our mother arrived home. She worked nights as a bartender at the Elks Club, so many nights we did not sleep much.

In the early years, I had very little identity aside from being the daughter who was angry with her alcoholic mother. She was a beautiful woman who made people laugh. She threw great bid whist parties and was a great friend to the people who surrounded her. She was an amazing cook and all together awesome to others. But to me, she was missing.

I managed my life around those sober moments when we could connect. When she was inebriated, I treated her horribly. Just awful. I had no control over her behavior, so I took control of mine. If she was drunk around me, as she often was at night, I ignored her. The more she came around me, the angrier I became. She wasn't doing anything purposely to annoy me, but I needed something she could not offer. I wanted moments of clarity, coherency, and bonding. She wanted quiet, reprieve, escape, rest, and idle chatter. She escaped through numbing herself exactly at the times I needed emotional stimulation. So I turned on her. I yelled at her to get away from me. Treating her so badly made me feel horrible inside, but seeing her that way felt far worse.

I continued to push her away until I was well into my thirties. Then when I was 35 and she was 55, she died. Her heart simply gave out.

There had been lots of pain. Lots of drunken birthday parties where I watered down her drinks so she would be with me, sober, longer. My friends loved and adored her, while I, on the other hand, stood on pins and needles. At Easter egg hunts, I prayed she would remember where she had hidden all the eggs because there was nothing as embarrassing as smelling forgotten boiled eggs that remained hidden under the porch in July.

For years, my mother and I spoke every single day, but we did not communicate very well. We had what I will call a passive-aggressive relationship. We never asked for what we needed from the other. We danced around it, painting word pictures in the air.

It was only after I married and had my first child that I began to realize how life happens. Momma lasted in life nearly eight years into my marriage. During those precious years, we steadily became best friends. At her core, she did not change one bit. I did.

Like Momma, I grew up in the church. Both my grandfathers pastored their own churches. My faith evolved from a very early age, and it remains deeply rooted and intensely personal. I have always talked to God. Sometimes, He was the only one in my house I spoke to. I had so much pain, and I was afraid that someone would see beyond my carefully-placed veil and see my pain up close. So I acted out, using humor mostly, to mask it. I made everything big. I was the class clown, and I did a lot to gain attention. I had my share of boyfriends, going from one to another until the day I married. From 15 until I turned 28, I was never without someone to call my man. Like my mother, I did not want to be alone.

No more, I told myself. If I was going to heal, I needed answers, lots of them. My pain clashing against my mother's pain was toxic. We were poised for attack, and our words turned hurtful if either of us felt the slightest bit of judgment from the other. She was more skilled at lethal outcomes. She knew that I would surrender quickly if wounded early, and she knew my softest, most vulnerable spots. At some point, I retreated. I pulled back this time, changing my weaponry. This time I used prayer. And before I traded words with her, I prayed for her, and I prayed for me. And after some time, something amazing happened. We fell in love.

Through continuous prayer, I had the opportunity to love my mother unconditionally in life and we both felt it. Sometimes in the middle of the night, I heard her weeping prayers from her room, always thanking God and praying for her children.

Many of the answers I needed, I got. But many more went to the grave with her. And in the end, I was okay with that.

We learned when to dance around topics that were uncomfortable. I learned to hear her intentions without judging her words. She saw that I needed her. As her eldest daughter, I wanted to be a part of her history, no matter how painful. So she let me in. Little by little, she let me peek into her soul. And because I had asked for it, I stayed there for only as long as I could stand it. It was scarred, dim and cracked. It had been through many battles, leaving a little piece on the battlefield each time. Like mine, her soul had seen more than its share of pain. In her, I saw me. And I sobbed.

For so long, I had been punishing her for trying to survive the best way she knew how. Now seeing inside her, I understood better. She carried pain from her relationship with her own mother. Again, I sobbed. Trying not to overstay my welcome, I backed out as gingerly as I had come in. I shut that door to her business and let her come to me when and if she chose to.

I have one daughter. I have given birth only once. Our son is adopted. It is solely because of my faith and my mother's willingness to let me sit at her feet and share what was on my heart that my spirit began to heal. I am not 100 percent, but I am emotionally healthy and strong. And I miss my mother tremendously.

I miss her like a daughter is supposed to miss her mom. I still talk to her. I used to smell her robe when I was lonely. I used to listen to her last voicemail on my cell phone over and over again. Though too small, I still wear the girdle she bought me, my first. I stayed in bed for two days when the electric skillet she bought me stopped working.

She was awesome; she was simple; and she had tremendous, unbridled love for me. Our relationship was complicated. We were so much alike. I lost my best friend and someone who gave so much of herself to save me from drowning.

I went on a mission trip in 2005. The experience changed my life. It was there, in rural Mississippi, that God spoke to me. He said simply, "Get over yourself." I knew exactly what He meant. And slowly and purposefully, I did.

The first thing I did was make things right with my mother, though she had been dead for three years already. I had to be okay with my mother in my head and in my heart. I had my own daughter to think about. I did not want history to repeat itself. Through a prayer channel, I asked my mother to forgive me for the way I had treated her when I was hurting the most, and I finally forgave myself.

I now understand.

This is my story, but it is not my life.

LA DETRA, SALT LAKE CITY, UT

My conception was a point of contention. My mother was married to my sister's father and having an affair with my father, a man married to another woman. The conflict was so great in her heart, she considered having an abortion. However, the way she told me the story was completely different. She said the doctors thought I was a tumor inside of her belly and wanted to cut me out of her stomach, but she wouldn't let them. As I became an adult, I learned she considered having an abortion but didn't go through with it. This is the first time God saved my life. He didn't let them kill me.

Two years later, my mother married another man that favored my biological father in looks, weight and height. She raised me as his child, telling me he was my biological father and even registering me in school with his last name, although he never adopted me. It wasn't until I was going to get my driver's license, and the clerk informed me that the name on my birth certificate was not the same. Imagine the shock of finding out the man listed on my birth certificate was fictitious. My mother made up the name on my birth certificate to hide the identity of my real father, who is a man I have never met or seen. In the state in which I was born if a woman was married at the time of a child's birth by law the child had to carry the last name of the husband.

I grew up in a two-parent household with a sister who hated me since birth, a mother trying her best to make her wrong look right, and a step-father that was mean as a hell. Though lies, hatred, jealousy and envy surrounded me, so did God. My mother believed in Jesus, but carried the shame of her mistakes. I remember going to church, praying, and hearing about Jesus.

What I don't remember was Jesus coming home with us, but I heard about the law every day. Everything I wanted to do was going to send me to hell quickly.

Self-hate bred in my brain like roaches in a dirty house. So many nights I would pray for God to take me in my sleep, because I didn't want to wake up to see another day of rejection, abandonment, lies and hatred. Every day I would wake up to memories of intense dreams. Dreams of a dark world full of death, demons and destruction. I would dream of a family member passing away, and only a few weeks later there would be a death in the family. When I told my mom about it, she would tell me I was a seer, meaning I could see into the spirit realm. She would think nothing of it and quote Joel 2:28, "Then, after doing all those things, I will pour out my Spirit upon all people. Your sons and daughters will prophesy. Your old men will dream dreams, and your young men will see visions." I was always confused, because she raised me in a church that didn't believe that the prophetic existed anymore.

I became just like my environment. I was a mean bully like my stepfather, wildly promiscuous like my mother, and hatefully vindictive like my sister. Then I discovered drugs. My oldest brother smoked weed with my mom, and she kept her stash in her underwear drawer. I had already started smoking cigarettes with my neighbor down the street, so when I found this funny looking cigarette, I didn't know what it was, but I knew I could smoke it. That is exactly what my friend, Tammy, and I did that next day. We laughed, joked and had fun that day after school. That was the most fun the two of us had. Tammy was a mean girl, too, and smoking weed soon became a regular occurrence for us. The weed made my dreams stop and deadened my pain. To me it was a win-win situation.

I smoked weed from the time I was 11 years old until my early thirties. I didn't just smoke weed, though. I tried every drug that didn't require a needle. Coke, crank, hash, pills, angel dust, sniff glue and primos (coke and weed mixed in a joint). The funny thing is after a short time of using coke, crank, angel dust or pills I would get sick as a dog, throwing up violently everywhere. I could never stay on a substance harder than weed for any extended period of time because of my stomach issues, making it impossible for me to become physically addicted. I believe this was God saving my life.

Just because I couldn't get addicted to drugs didn't mean I couldn't sell it. I connected with an older drug dealer in the Bay Area and started selling drugs in my high school. My parents were very well-known in that little military town, so I couldn't sell it directly. I had a few guys in high school selling it for me, which was the beginning of my dual lifestyle: drug dealer and corporate businesswoman. My mother kicked me out when I was 15, and I dropped out of high school for a corporate job in the eleventh grade. It seemed that everywhere I went, I always ended up connecting with a drug dealer who would give me weight (drugs in quantity) for a really low price.

I wasn't the type to be slanging it on the corner, but there were always some corporate executives looking to score without going to the hood. I continued selling drugs and climbing the corporate ladder for all of my early adult life with no resemblance of God in my life. At 17, I had started living with my married military boyfriend. At 18, we were both baptized. Shortly thereafter, my pastor told me I needed to stop living with him and walk in the ways of the Lord. At that point, I turned my back on God and started dancing with the devil full swing. At 19, I moved to Los Angeles, and I have only one memory of ever stepping foot in a church during my time there.

Thanks to my drug use, I hadn't had dreams for years. I was living my life footloose and fancy free – doing what I wanted with whom I wanted, when I wanted. Then I had a dream of the worst intensity. I dreamed my mother died. This shook my world because I knew dreams of death are a warning of things to come. My mother was my rock! She was all I had, the only person who loved me unconditionally and was always there for me. When my siblings discarded me and my father never looked for me, she loved me, encouraged me and reminded me that no matter how far I ran from God, Jesus still loved me and all things would come to pass.

I called my mom following her outpatient procedure, and we talked for hours as usual. She explained what it was like to be on a morphine drip the different kind of high it produced. I was startled, because they don't give morphine for everyday outpatient surgery. Since my mother had a history of operating in deception, I called my stepfather. He cosigned my mother's explanation, though I didn't believe him either. I reminded him of who I was – a drug dealer with precision shooting skills, I promised to fly to Arkansas and put a bullet between his eyes if I found out he was lying to me and something happened to my mother. With that threat, he told me my mother was living with a terminal lung disease that was getting worse fast.

I left Los Angeles and went to Arkansas to be with my mother. I hadn't been there for two weeks when she had a heart attack one morning after my stepfather left for work at 5 o'clock a.m. I am not a morning person, but that morning, I woke up early and was shocked to find my mom still sleeping. At 9 a.m., I tried to wake her for work, but she barely responded. Her eyes rolled back in her head, and her speech was slurred. My stepfather returned home and took her to the hospital, where the doctor diagnosed right-sided heart failure due to her lung disease. She had suffered a heart attack in her sleep and would have died had she not received medical attention when she did. A year later, she died of another heart attack, going to her grave with the truth about my biological father and not knowing if any of her children would ever give their lives to Christ.

Between the first and second heart attacks, I stayed as high as I could possibly get. I took some college courses, took care of my mom, fought frequently with my stepfather and begged for my siblings to visit our mother before she died. I never finished that degree, and they never came. I did, however; fall in love with my local drug dealer. He was handsome, smart and a man's man who was sweet on me. He worked a full-time job, went to school full-time and wanted to be a doctor. Prior to him, I never wanted to settle down and get married. My mother had five kids, five husbands, and four divorces, so commitment didn't mean much to me. I just wanted to be footloose and fancy free. He loved me in a way that I hadn't experienced before. He affirmed me, challenged me, and was there for me like no one else had ever been. Following my mother's death, he kept me alive as I attempted to starve myself. He forced me to eat. He believed in me, and his love for me never diminished, no matter how close he got to me.

What I didn't know was he was a recovering crack addict on a fast road to relapse. By the time I realized I couldn't love him out of his addiction, it was too late. I was pregnant. I cried my whole first trimester. I was stuck. My back was against the wall, and I was going to be responsible for another life! My mother had been gone six months, so I had no one to go to for help and advice. Then I remembered my mother's words of wisdom: No matter how far you run from God, Jesus still loves you, and this too will come to pass.

During my pregnancy, I began to read my Bible again. Although I didn't always understand what I was reading, I always felt at peace while reading it. Then I started going back to church occasionally. The closer I got to God, the more volatile my situation became. After having my baby, my crack addict boyfriend turned violent. I remember him choking me once outside of a casino, and another time throwing me across the room because I wouldn't give him money to go smoke crack for the weekend. The final straw was when he slammed me against the wall, snatched my leather purse and ripped it in half, taking the rent money. He threw the apartment keys at me so hard that they cut my neck. Then, he left to go smoke.

I slid down that wall and cried out to God, "How did I get here?" God replayed the mistakes I had made over the course of my life – drug deals, drug use, multiple lovers, and a host of poor decisions. He showed me time after time, where I had chosen the ways of the world over the ways of the Lord. In that moment, I prayed, "God, if you will deliver me from this, I will serve you all the days of my life."

In the course of a weekend, I watched God move miraculously on my behalf. He delivered provision, protection, and favor. I packed up everything in that little one-bedroom apartment, gathered up my two month old baby boy, and headed for Atlanta, Georgia, in the middle of the night.

My life has never been the same. The Holy Spirit walked me through years of sanctification, and I am proud to say I am 12 years drug-free. Now, I have the awesome opportunity to serve Christ through marketplace ministry, in my local church, and in my personal life coaching business, Breakthroughforlife.com. I am single and raising a young boy into a God- fearing man. That bouncing baby boy is junior at a local, private, Christian school and is a straight-A honor student and member of the National Honor Society. He plays the violin and is the concertmaster in his high school orchestra. His greatest passion is singing songs of worship to his personal Lord and Savior, Jesus Christ. He is fully aware of all God has delivered me from, the struggle his father suffered through, and the power of Christ to redeem the lost. I always tell him, "Your father was a good man with a bad habit."

We are not a perfect family, but we are acutely aware of our need for a savior every day. God is faithful if we are willing. My troubled childhood and turbulent early adulthood can only define me if I allow it.

This is my story, but it is not my life.

BRENDA, ATLANTA, GA

FAMILY AND
RELATIONSHIPS

I am an addict. I have been for as long as I can remember. I suppose you do not think an 8 year old can be an addict, but I was. No, it was not drugs, not alcohol; certainly not gambling or sex, but an addiction just as devastating...an addiction just as sinister...one that would cause me to lose my home, my car, my credit, my self-esteem. One I resorted to in order to ease the anger and pain stored inside me, one fed by my fears of rejection and abandonment; one that caused me to lie to family and friends, to leave projects and goals unfinished, and to compromise my values.

My addiction is people-pleasing, the deep emotional need to make people like me, love me, befriend me. My high has been the thrill of being accepted and valued, being treated special, being noticed. I'm sweet, energetic, and giving, so you're probably thinking, "Doesn't sound so bad. Everyone likes to be accepted and valued, right?" Maybe, but I thought I needed it. In fact, I craved it. Without others' acceptance, I was nothing. Alone with my own thoughts, I often questioned, "Who am I really? Do I even know who I am? Do I even love myself?"

I am a product of teenage love. My parents started dating in their early teens and were married shortly thereafter. I arrived when they were only 16 and 19. My father was in college; my mother worked. While most teenagers cannot handle the responsibility of a child, and having a baby practically destroys their lives, my parents determinedly did whatever needed to be done. Together, they provided a good home for me and gave me the very best they could afford.

My parents had been chosen and called to be worshipers for Christ. My father was called to preach at a young age, but to provide for us, he also worked a second job, causing him to work long hours. He did his best to be there for us, but his dissatisfaction with his work life bled over into our family life. His rejection became our rejection. As time passed, his unhappiness ate into the peace of our family, just like the cancer that would later eat away at my body.

Rejection was not new in our family history. It has been like an unwanted vine wrapped all up in my family tree, twisted through the roots of our past generations and handed down like a poisonous legacy. Our family's way of coping has always been to stay busy. The busier we are, the deeper we can bury the hurt. Perhaps because of this, my childhood left me with a void I have felt all my life, a longing for something more, a need to be filled, fertile ground for my addiction.

As daughter of a preacher, my life revolved around home, school, and church, especially church. In our house, unless we were practically on our death bed, the rule was, "You are going to church." We were there every time the church doors opened. I remember the day I accepted Christ into my life when I was 8 years old. On that particular Sunday morning, when our pastor was asking who wanted to join the body of Christ and be baptized, I jumped up like I was on fire, without any hesitation. I came forward to sit in a chair up front. A strong presence came over me. For a moment, everything went silent in my head. I was the only one who came forward that Sunday morning. Seven chairs were in the front of the church next to me and sat empty. I sat in the eighth chair. Eight is the number of new beginnings. Tears in my father's eyes spoke loudly to me that day. I was happy and excited for this decision in my life, and I knew he was proud. I felt loved.

Even though accepting Christ changed my life and I knew I was different, I still had to deal with normal life. As a child, I was mercilessly bullied. My fix was to use my quick wit and personality to get people to accept me. As I grew, I even showered people with gifts, so my life would be better and I could avoid rejection. Even though I had accepted Christ and felt anointed by God, I selfishly ran from His plans for me and His help. Wanting to be accepted by others was more important to me. It became my primary focus; my quick-fix; my addiction. As long as everyone praised me, I was happy; but as soon as I found myself alone without the high of praise and acceptance, I had to go find others to get my next fix.

People-pleasing became my new way of life. I spent the rest of my childhood, as well as my teenage and early adult years, indulging my addiction and falling deeper into its web of lies. I moved to Atlanta at 23 years old. My career as a manager of flight attendants was full, and I lived it up! On the outside, my life looked good. People accepted me, respected me, praised me. Inside, however, I felt empty. Living in this world to please others, I had mastered the spirit of manipulation. I was a queen of deception, and the person I deceived the most was myself. I had no direction, other than my addiction. It consumed my waking hours. You may say, "So, lots of 20-somethings are like that." Not like this. I did not know who I was anymore. You see, when you entertain one negative spirit, it brings others to create even more havoc. I wasn't faithful with finances, not paying bills on time. I even lied to my mother and told her my life was great in Atlanta, at a time when I was facing eviction and the loss of my car.

Even worse was my personal dating life. I was in relationship after relationship, addicted to the need to be loved, with each man leaving me even more broken. You create soul ties with everyone with whom you connect. By doing so, you allow them to deposit something into your life. Some deposits are not put there by God and are harmful to you. I knew God was telling me to change my ways and be careful, but I was having fun. Everyone liked me. I was free, happy, and living on my own. Full speed ahead!

God had to put a stop to this madness. One night, as I was leaving a dance club, I drove by a brightly lit church, and a presence overtook me. A voice said, "It's time. Come here tomorrow and get your freedom back." I don't know why, but I started crying and could not stop. I don't think I slept at all that night. That very next morning, I got up, got dressed, attended that church and felt a renewed sense of blessing. I joined, immediately becoming active. It was exciting to feel new changes taking place in my life. The pastor and his wife took me under their wings, as if I was one of their own. I ended up working for the church and renting a house it owned. I began to believe God really did love me, which gave me strength to fight for a better life.

My life started looking up, but my faithful, old addiction still had a hold on me. When I met a young, smooth-talking pastor who pursued me and treated me like a lady, my desire to be accepted and loved opened the door to lust. I turned a blind eye and deaf ear again to God, ignoring the warnings of my new pastor, to begin an inappropriate relationship with this man. Addicted to the need to be loved, I gave all of myself to him. Because of this relationship, I ended up being homeless, lost my car, and spent nights sleeping at friends' houses. I even lied to this man as to my dire financial situation, because I was afraid of rejection. I desperately did not want him to leave me. Thankfully, God intervened again. He sent my grandmother a dream in which He told her to come from Ohio to get me, as I was in danger. When Saturday morning came; I heard a car horn honking outside. There sat my mother and grandmother in the car. They had come to take me back to Ohio. Funny thing is, I didn't get mad or argue. I packed my stuff and got in the car. Even though part of me was sad, I felt like a weight had been lifted off me. Peace washed over me.

God knew I needed my family. I soon discovered I was pregnant with the young pastor's child, and that the man wanted nothing more to do with me or our baby. My fear of abandonment and rejection multiplied tenfold. I had just moved back home with my parents; and I had a temporary job with no money saved. Afraid, but strong, I accepted I would be a single mother. I started making plans. Then, the week he was due, my beautiful and much loved son was stillborn. Boom! A bomb exploded inside my heart and soul. My mind went numb at this news. Total black silence overtook me. I could hear and feel nothing, yet my body let out a loud, continuous scream for more than 15 minutes, until they gave me something to knock me out. Later, when I woke up, I felt that God was telling me He loved me very much and that sometimes people die so that others may be saved through God's love. I told my mother I knew God was trying to save me. I was His baby, too. Even so, tears fell for hours as I dealt with the pain of another person leaving me. Nothing eased my pain.

Things seemed to go from bad to worse. Six months after the devastation of my son's death, at my checkup, I learned I had cancer. I needed surgery before the cancer spread. Again, my mind went numb as the doctor spoke. He gave me a book to read about the type of cancer I had. It said I only had five years to live. I couldn't speak, even though a thousand thoughts ran through my mind. How could this be? I was only 26 years old. I had just started living. All I had ever wanted was to be loved. I had just carried a baby who could have loved me, but I had to bury him. That had been a death blow. Now cancer? How will I ever know love now? How can this be happening? Suddenly, I rediscovered my voice. I let out a primal scream, right in the doctor's office. It was my battle cry.

I finally realized I needed God more than I ever knew. I said, "God, this can't be it for me. You promised more for me in Your Word." My mother, being the prayer warrior she is, said to me, "You put that packet down, and don't ever pick it up to read it again. We will beat this." With that, we started my journey to being whole. Ever since that day in the doctor's office, God has healed me emotionally and physically. Fear is a deadly disease. What no one knows for real, until they really sit and spend time with God and lets Him show them, is all the dirty things Satan tries to use to destroy you. I learned to love myself, because God loves me as I am. I thank God daily that I can say, "Here I am now at 44 years old. The cancer has never returned." God has blessed me with a wonderful husband of six years. He has never judged me, and he accepts me and loves me as I am.

Yes, I was addicted to people and needed their acceptance to feel fulfilled. Yes, my family has a legacy of rejection and its pain, but I found healing. I will forever trust God for everything and if He says, "Move," I'll move. I now know that it may just cost me everything if I don't.

Now, when I think I need others' acceptance and praise, or my addiction tugs at me, instead of following that self-destruction demon, I hear my God say:

"I call you Beauty!
Beautiful you are to Me, filled with Eternity;
All that you went through was to unveil the real you;
The more I pushed, the more you pressed through;
Don't ever question My love for you.

For it is real and true.
The sacrifice I gave was My Only Son;
Oh too well you now know that pain.
My kisses to you are like the morning sun;
I wiped your tears that fell down like rain.
I raise you up to shine and be free in Me;
So that others will know I am waiting for them;
For my deep, pure love and grace they cannot see.
My beautiful, beautiful daughter, stand tall, stand proud;
For it is now, I release you into the crowd.
Show them My love is real and cannot be broken.
Everlasting and so much richer than any temporary earthly token."

This is my story but it is not my life.

TONYA RENEE, CINCINNATI, OH

I grew up in a protective environment, though I was never really sure what or who I was being protected from. Ours was a day by day existence. We grew up fast and close. It was the four of us children against the world.

In my family, I was a real standout because I preferred school and grades to running the streets. Of course, I did my share of sneaking out to dance clubs after Momma stepped out or was at work. I was nowhere near perfect, but no matter what I tried – beauty pageants, oratorical contests, fashion shows, modeling, whatever – I always had their full support.

Our house was the gathering spot, simply because my mother worked nights. We created a lot of mischief in that house only to restore the house to order whenever we heard Momma's car or she called to say she was on her way home.

My brothers were ultra-protective of my sister and me. They were the men of the house when Momma was away at work. My brothers often brought their friends around. Without fail, if they had friends over, there was going to be a fight or scuffle, generally about me or my sister.

We lived in a small house, so nearly everything happened in the front room or our bedrooms. I usually did my homework in the front room. My brother, Wade, was notorious for fighting in that front room, typically because someone looked at me or said something out of order.

"Don't even look at her, man. I mean it. Don't ask me about her either. Don't look her way. Act like you don't even see her sitting there. Fair warning. One warning."

I kept my eyes glued to my book, pretending to be studying even as I knew what inevitably awaited. By the time I could count to about four, one or more of his friends would look my way. Then Pow! It was full on tussle right there in the front room. My self-appointed job was to move stuff that, if broken, would get us all in trouble, e.g., TV, cassette player, pictures of Jesus, cheap African statues, whatnot.

Some of his same friends got into a fight with Wade over harmless looking every time they came over. I've never been entirely sure whether Wade did not play when it came to his sisters or he just liked to fight. Either way, it was crazy, and he fought a lot.

Once, Wade begged me to set up a movie double-date with my prettiest friend, Kina. She was Halle Berry-beautiful. After I promised her the world in return, she finally relented. My brother ran home after his cooking shift at a fast food restaurant to change and meet us there. I smelled his Old Spice from a mile away. Midway through the movie, he asked me to join him in the lobby. He asked, "What does she think of me? Am I making a good impression? Tell the truth." He prodded for five minutes.

Frustrated that we were missing the movie, I blurted out, "She says you smell like hamburgers."

He stood frozen in place. He teared up, this fighter from our front room. He demanded, "Smell me," pulling me into his shirt and his over-abundance of Old Spice cover up.

I lied and said, "Just a little. Not really." We returned to the movie, Kina sitting oblivious between us. Wade cried in his chair, and I cried in mine, silent, sad, angry tears from each of us. Neither of us cared about the movie or Kina. It was us against the world. Never again did I fix him up. And I didn't have to.

The day I graduated from high school, I became the first in my immediate family to do so. My older brothers chose differently. I remember being chosen to give the senior class commencement address. Upon finishing, I saw someone standing alone in the balcony wearing a McDonald's uniform. It was my brother Wade, leading a standing ovation. He was as proud as though he had delivered the remarks himself. I will never forget that day.

The day I left for Howard University, my brother Wade was there. I remember vividly him running up to the taxi that had come to collect me curbside from our tiny house in Salt Lake City, Utah. Momma could not collect herself long enough to see me walk to the taxi. She was overcome with a balance of pride and sadness that I was leaving her. But Wade was there. He had always been there. As I got seated in the back of the taxi, he said, "Hey wait a minute. Get out! Do you know how... to fight?"

I was only half-stunned. That was his way, always looking out for me. He made me get out of the taxi long enough to learn how to get the first punches and to protect my face. The poor taxi driver sat there stunned, perhaps even wowed by my high school dropout older brother preparing me for college.

As the taxi pulled away from the curb, he said, "Here, take this wooden nickel, and make damn sure it is the last one you ever take." Little did I know, throughout the next 35 years, the tables would turn. I would repeatedly save Wade.

Though we all grew up in the same environment, its effect was more harsh on Wade. He seemed to feel things more deeply. He was and is super-sensitive, quietly compassionate. He has never met a stranger and is a friend to the world around him. He is naïve and street smart at once. Just 21 months older than me, he was my mother's favorite. She used to always say he needed her more. Likely he did.

I remember him being held back a year, which put us in the same second grade class. It almost killed him. He was humiliated. And over the years, we would grow apart. I took the so-called right path, while Wade went left. What brought us back together was a call from my sister. Wade was in the hospital, and the doctors were not sure they could save his life. My first response was anger, because I knew bad behavior and poor choices were responsible for his condition. Still, I jumped on a plane. He was my brother, my family. I had already buried my mother to a heart condition and my other brother, who succumbed to cancer at 45. As the oldest living child, I had to see about him. What I found nearly killed me.

As I entered the hospital room where he had already spent the better part of two months, the first thing I noticed was his emaciation. The strong handsome twin of my mother was gone, long lost to the streets. He appeared frail, desperate, sad and weak. This brother who so many years ago taught me to fight, looked as though all of his fight was gone. He looked up at me through his methadone haze and managed a weak smile. I refused to cry, but inside I wailed. Seeing my brother lying there in a million little pieces broke me. Where on earth was I going to begin to help? I hoped just by being there was a mighty first step.

Over the next several days, he shared his version of how it had come to this. He had been homeless and in and out of prison for twenty-plus years, both of which I knew. That he had collapsed in a friend's back yard from pain in his spine was somewhat of a surprise to me. It was rainy, windy, and cool when his friend lifted him into his car and dropped him at the hospital, where the doctors were using their finest technology to save his life.

Wade had a staph infection that was not responding to any antibiotics. The bacteria was attacking his bones and organs with a vengeance, and if the final antibiotic didn't work, he would die. The odds were stacked against him. All 23 of the last patients the hospital had seen with similar symptoms died. When I dropped off my rental car to return home, I told my story to the rental agent. She cried. She had lost her brother six months before at the same hospital. He died of a staph infection.

There was nothing I could do, other than give it all to God. So with my brother's consent, I shared his story and asked others to pray with me. There are a lot of Wades out there. I am not alone. I talk about it not to sensationalize it, but to begin the healing process for me and others like me.

When I left my brother, he asked me to buy him a pack of cigarettes. I refused because I love him too much. I knew that someone else would. A few, not many, people stopped by to visit him while I was with him. I would not allow any negative talk. My brother knows better than anyone the hole he has dug for himself. He does not need to be reminded or criticized. "Not today," I said. "Not around me." I could not allow it.

Only time will tell how Wade's story will end. I left him with $25, a smile and a hug. Choking back tears, I said, "I am family, and I will never leave you."

He asked, "You promise?"

"I promise."

I am not ready to bury my brother, and with God's help, I won't have to. I believe in the holy trinity. I believe God when he says prayer changes things. My faith is placed at the altar believing that God is sovereign. He will do what He said He will do. If only we believe.

This is my story, but it is not my life.

JOY, FLINT, MICHIGAN

I love mosaic art. I always have. As I look back over my life and how far I have come, God has blessed me with the beautiful picture of my life as one great piece of mosaic art. To create a piece of mosaic art, you collect small broken or fragmented pieces of colored glass and arrange them strategically to create a beautiful piece of art. This is what God has done in my life. For years, I defined myself as broken to define myself, my emotions, and my actions. There were parts of my life that felt fragmented and shattered. It wasn't until recently that God brought me full circle and told me that although I had been broken, I made a beautiful mosaic picture of my life. I never knew rejection was a spirit so strong it could cripple a person before birth. But I know it now, because I experienced my father's rejection at the time of birth. The relationship between my mother and father was extremely volatile. My father was an alcoholic, and my home life was filled with lots of arguing. After one particularly bad argument, I remember my mother telling me that my father didn't want me, that he wasn't at the hospital when I was born. Deep sadness came over me. I couldn't believe my father didn't want me, that he wasn't concerned about me. My mother meant to hurt me. She was hurting, too. She was speaking from a place of pain, because she was suffering through the same situation as I was. I was a child not receiving the love I yearned for, and she was a wife dealing with a deep void. This revelation was the beginning of a life long struggle of trying to gain the love and acceptance of a man. Although my dad was present physically in our home, he was very distant emotionally. Not being able to understand that alcohol had control over his life and was what caused him to be distant, I came to the conclusion that it was because he didn't love me. I longed for my father to be active in my life. I wanted a father who would come to father-daughter breakfasts at school and all of the other activities that I participated in. It was so lonely to sit there and see other girls with their dads and wonder why mine didn't want to be there. There is a special place in a little girl's heart that only a father can touch, and mine was empty. I longed for his love, and the tragedy was that because I didn't receive it, I sought it out from other men.

In college, I became very promiscuous in an effort to fill the void. When the first guy showed me any attention, I was ready to do anything to keep that attention. This is what I had wanted for years and now that I had experienced it, my goal was to keep it by any means necessary. What I didn't understand is that there are broken men in this world who will say and do anything to get what they want from you. I thought that they wanted me and all of the love I had to share, but many only wanted a moment of pleasure before moving on to the next conquest. As this happened time and time again, I was left feeling devastated and even emptier than before. Each time, a little piece of me broke off, and I wondered if I would ever be whole again. I didn't realize that never-ending rejection was spiraling me further down into low self-esteem and self-hatred. Not only was I dealing with the rejection that I experienced at the hands of the men who came in and out of my life, but I was now rejecting myself. I was nervous about the names that others were calling me, but the voice within my own head was the loudest and most critical of them all. Really, it didn't matter what others said about me, because I whispered the worst things to myself: whore, slut, easy. I started telling myself I was damaged goods. Love of a man, the thing I wanted most, seemed even farther away. I wondered who would want me. My fear was no good man would.

But God. He saw me, and He wanted to heal me and bring my broken pieces back together. During my freshman year in college, a friend I had known since high school began encouraging me to go to church. I had attended a Christian school when I was young, so I knew of God. I had learned a lot about Him over my lifetime, but there was one important thing missing and that was the relationship. When I was growing up, we attended church mainly for special occasions and holidays. It was my sophomore year when I finally surrendered my life to Christ, and God began to do a work within me. He told me nothing I had done, or ever could do, would change His love for me. My heavenly Father loved me in spite of everything I had done.

On the day I surrendered to Christ, I began the most important journey of my life. When you give your life to Christ, everything doesn't instantly change and become great forever. Not that God cannot do it that way, but most times, it's a day-to-day process to overcome and make peace with the struggles you have faced throughout life. I have learned I will continually grow and get better. I am still a work in progress today, and I understand the reason why God's mercies are new each day. It's because I need His mercy, grace, and love each and every day.

The biggest struggle I have had is learning to love myself. The internal damage far outweighed the external problems. If a train has been traveling in one direction at a high rate of speed for a long time, it will take time to stop the train, turn it around, and start it traveling in a new direction. It takes time to reprogram your mind and the thoughts that have been floating around for years. The voice of negativity was not easy to silence, and it still speaks at times. The difference between then and now is I am able to recognize the voice and can combat it with the Word of God. When the voice says that I am not good enough, I say that I am fearfully and wonderfully made. When the voice says I'm going to fail, I say all things are possible through Christ Jesus. When the voice tells me my life will not have purpose, I say that God knows the plans He has for me to give me a hope and a future. And when the voice says I have no direction, I say when I trust and acknowledge God and don't lean on my own understanding, He will direct my path. I have learned that I can use the Word of God to combat every attack.

Over the years, as my life in Christ has become stronger, I have begun to see myself for who I really am. I am a child of the most high God and daughter of the King. I was perfectly made in His image. God created me, and there were no mistakes in His craftsmanship. God has, and continues to, come between me and all of the lies I have told myself. Each day, I continue on my journey toward fully loving and accepting myself, but I am grateful to have God by my side every step of the way. There may be up days and down days, but I am grateful for the progress I have made, and I am assured He that has begun a good work in me and will finish it. God's love, grace and mercy have been instrumental in me becoming who I am today. I have fully embraced the victory I have through Christ Jesus and the blood He shed for me on Calvary. There is nothing that can separate me from the love of God, because He loved me even when I didn't love myself.

I am blessed to say that before my father departed this earth, God reconciled us, and the last words we spoke to each other were, "I love you." God has also blessed me with a wonderful husband, who is fully aware of my past and loves me anyway. He is a visible reflection of God's unconditional love for me. My freedom in Christ allows me to share my story without any guilt or shame. God has taken all of the broken pieces and made a beautiful piece of art. My goal in life is to share my story so that others understand you do not have to suffer in silence and remain broken. If you offer God your life, even if it has been shattered into pieces, He will take what you give Him and make it beautiful. When I look in the mirror, I am proud of the woman I see. I am stronger because of my journey. And the wonderful thing is that God is not done yet…

This is my story, but it is not my life.

VAGILLA, ATLANTA, GA

STARTING OVER

It was 1:39 a.m. I thought I had heard a cell phone ring earlier, but I was disoriented and thought I was dreaming. Several minutes later, my husband tapped me on the shoulder and passed me his phone. Dazed, I looked at the name, and the fact that no one calls at that time of morning unless something is wrong went over my head. I managed a groggy, "Hello????" The words that followed still make my ears ring.

In a voice as calm as one can imagine, my sister said, "I need you to wake up and listen to me. We just received word that Innocence was shot and killed last night, and I need you to go identify his body." I fell to the floor, the world spinning uncontrollably, the bowels of my belly ferociously twisting, and my head reeling in pain. I felt as though I had been hit. I thought I would vomit, but it stuck in my throat, choking me. I prayed silently, Lord, please help me breathe!

My husband knelt next to me. I was inconsolable. Certainly, I was dreaming. Certainly my sister had not just calmly told me her son, my nephew who had been living with me for almost a year, had been shot and killed.

Eleven months earlier, my sister, Kim, called to say Innocence wanted to come to live with me to work out with a professional trainer to get ready to re-enter a professional sport – one in which he was projected to be one of America's greatest. Of course, he could come. I helped raise him. I called him my own at times. I was his favorite auntie. He hugged and kissed me without reserve. He was genuine, innocent, and pure. He had hopes and dreams of greatness and of making his family and entire community proud. His eyes danced when the corners of his lips turned up in a smile, and his body shook the earth when he laughed, because it came from deep within. It had been three years since I had seen much of him, because he was away preparing for greatness when an injury sidelined him. But I welcomed him with open arms.

After a few weeks, I realized the person who showed up on my doorstep was different from the Innocence I remembered. He was empty and broken. The air around him was dark. A back injury led to painkillers and other narcotics. His stare was blank. I had kids in their tender years – sons who worshipped him. He couldn't stay. "You've got to go!!!" I screamed.

After countless fights, arguments, and threats, Innocence finally looked at me with tears in his eyes. He put his hands on my shoulders and with solemn resolve, said, "Help me." He meant it.

At 47-years-old, I had never once seen any drugs – not even marijuana. I was conflicted with offering the protection I owed my kids versus turning my back on a pure heart that was crying out for help. He needed me, and I would be there. We began to have long talks. He went two months clean. It was hard. His hands would shake. At first, he was irritable, but he was committed. He said he didn't need rehab, but he agreed to go to counseling – once. The air of darkness around him lifted. He was engaged with my family. The old Innocence was returning slowly. I called my sister and brother-in-law to tell them he was doing well. They thanked me from the bottom of their hearts, and inside I felt myself gloating as if I had done something. My sister is literally the most spiritual person I know. She lay on the altar for him. Both she and her husband awoke daily at 4 a.m. to pray on his behalf. They fasted weekly to stir up their zeal, renew their faith, and draw closer to God. They prayed for his deliverance. But I – lowly and unrighteousness – took credit for fixing him.

The darkness reappeared. I knew he was drifting. He couldn't look me in the eyes. He'd walk in the house and quickly retreat to the basement. I felt helpless. I needed to rescue him, to fix him, to do something, anything, to bring restore him. I couldn't tell my sister he had drifted again. I just couldn't bring myself to hurt her, but she knew. He came from her womb. He hurt from the disappointment and pain he brought to his mother. I couldn't tell her, but she always knew. I had to fix it, fix him, for her.

For months, he struggled. Finally, I had all I could take. Before I knew it or thought it through, I told him he had to go. He showed up that morning at 2 a.m. with a hollowed darkness I had never seen before. He looked like death. I didn't know what to do, and I was scared. Four days later, Innocence was gone. Shot and killed. Dead.

It was my fault. I shouldn't have kicked him out. When my sister insisted on coming to have him involuntarily committed to rehab two days before, I said he would be fine. The day he was killed, they had been planning to help move him into his own place. It could wait. He would be okay, I implored. He hated me. He could not believe I had kicked him out.

Several times during their long drive to my house, I spoke with my sister. Each time, she had a steady calmness that was odd. When she arrived, I wanted to fall to my knees before her and beg for her forgiveness for failing her. I couldn't. She never allowed space for it. She walked in with a kiss and a tight hug, and said, "I love you!"

How could she? Your child died on my watch, I thought. You sent him here to keep him focused and out of trouble. How can you love me? I kicked him out in the cold from anger. You should hate me. How can I ever look you in the eyes again? Hit me! Yell at me! Kick me, but please don't pretend you love me!

I could not cry in front of her. When she left the room, I would immediately lose it. I would flail wildly on the floor. I beat walls and cried profusely. When she entered, I turned it off and put on a face that was not one reeling in pain. My brother-in-law was practically comatose. He would manage a few words, but she was our strength.

Once, she caught me uncomposed. I was kneeling and rocking in place. She knelt down and said to me, "God cannot fail. I birthed Innocence, but I gave all of my children to God, and if this was His way of healing him, then Amen."

Amen? Amen? My brother-in-law had prayed the night before, "Lord, please just give my son peace." What faith they had!

For four months, I lived through an inexplicable depression. I couldn't sleep, but at the same time, I could hardly lift my head off my pillow. I didn't eat. Everything around me suffered, especially my family. I watched 1:39 a.m. pass on the clock every morning. I listened for his voice. I saw him. I smelled him. I argued and fought with him. I hated him.

My healing didn't start until one day when my sister called, and I was drowning. Once again, I was giving a heart-wrenching and introspective dissertation on how I was supposed to fix my nephew in the same manner I fixed everything and everyone. In the same quiet, calm voice, she said, "But you can't fix God". Her words hit me like a ton of bricks. In my head, I was entrusted to save Innocence from himself. But I had not gone to God as his intercessor. How dare I! What had I done for almost twelve months other than nothing? Then, her "But you can't fix God" had me gasping for air in the midst of already trying to heal from his devastating loss. How selfish and arrogant of me to think I could fix him. Was I even trying to do it for him or was it for me to prove that, once again, I could do it? I put way too much faith in my own nothingness when only God is sovereign.

Ten months later, I received a call from a new client. Her 19-year-old daughter had been shot and killed. My client, Lucky, refers to herself as a retired drug dealer. I have learned so much from Lucky in such a short time. She knows God. She retired about nine years ago after she promised God to never sell drugs again, if He allowed her to get out of jail and raise her children. She promised to go back to her roots and develop a relationship with God like her grandmother's. She was released after serving a few months of a 10-year sentence. She was penniless, but she never looked back to her old life.

Lucky unknowingly ministers to me every time we talk. Not once has she ever questioned God. She said she was sent to be raised by her grandmother after being molested for years by her stepfather and stepbrother, who fathered her child. While living with her grandmother, she witnessed what she called "that crazy faith." She said she was constantly looking to disprove her grandmother's faith. When she couldn't disprove it, she began to pray to have it. Lucky put Innocence's death into perspective, and I thank her. I thank God.

She said when Satan couldn't tempt her with drugs, he was constantly looking to disprove her faith in other ways. She said she didn't know she actually had that crazy faith until her daughter died. Because of her, I saw Innocence as God's child, and I began to release the guilt and heaviness.

If before Innocence arrived, someone told me I would be coexisting in my house with an addict, I would have responded with bold incredulity. I was too well put together for that. No one of that ilk, even family, was deserving of my time, let alone sharing my space. In my own head, I allowed myself to believe my problems had airs of sophistication. I was a fool to even think such a thing. My nephew needed me. He asked for help. Once I told him I prayed God would not give him any rest as long as he was doing wrong. He told me my prayers had been answered because his spirit was in constant turmoil. He did not die from anything drug-related, but that doesn't matter, because he's still gone. He was in the wrong place at the wrong time.

I have learned through my healing that my sister grieved, but she would not allow me to see her brokenness, because she never wanted me to carry one second of guilt. I was angry at God, because it didn't make sense to me that her child would die such a horrible death. She is His true servant. None of us can answer why it happened, but she believes from the depths of her soul that God does not make mistakes. She was God's vessel for Innocence, but Innocence was His. She raised him in the church, both the physical edifice and in their committed spirits. She doesn't fake religion or practice it part-time; she lives for Jesus. I wanted that relationship with God – that crazy faith that defies logic.

I've heard time and time again that addiction is a disease. Whoever figured that out was right. It's a cruel disease that I now see no differently than cancer, Alzheimer's, diabetes, or AIDS. Its victims are our mothers and fathers, sisters and brothers, nieces and nephews, our friends. They deserve our love. They need our compassion. We must free ourselves of the shame we carry when someone has fallen victim to drugs. That's their cross. We each have our own demons of equivalence. They are never sophisticated. Their purpose is set – to kill, steal, and destroy. My demons – like everyone else – were meant for evil. Instead, I thank God they led me to a crazy faith that sustains me.

This is my story, but it is not my life.

MONIQUE, ATLANTA, GA

94

I was named after Queen Esther in the Bible, but I have not always felt like a queen. I had a wonderful childhood. God had His hand on me even before I was born. I was adopted when I was a week old. My adoptive mother told the story that they received a call that a baby was ready for adoption. When she told my adoptive father, he said the baby was not the baby for them. So they waited; they waited for me. I was brought up in a very loving home. My parents raised me in the church, and it was my sweet mother who led me to the Lord at the age of 13 after I heard a message on Hell. I was a very quiet child and even though my parents loved me with an unconditional love and believed in me, I at times felt insecure and not very confident.

After graduating from high school, I went to college to study to be a teacher. I never had a boyfriend in high school, so when a Christian boy who was studying to be a preacher took interest in me, I knew this was right. I did not pray about it or seek God's will. I was a Christian, and he was a Christian so everything was meant to be, I thought.

Things were fine at first, but I started noticing that he was controlling, and when I did something he did not like, he would let me know very harshly. There was some pushing and firm grips on the arms. But what did the most damage to me was the verbal and emotional abuse. I did not have much confidence in myself, and I really felt worthless when I did something that was not up to my boyfriend's expectations. I walked on egg shells. I did not want to do anything that would set him off. Living like that day in and day out makes your self-worth very low. It was a vicious cycle. I was trying to be the wonderful girlfriend, but deep down I thought I was dumb, stupid, and worthless. When you hear often that you can't do anything right, you start believing it. I was in church every week, but I was not in the Bible like I should have been. As I have learned through all my trials, you must read and build yourself up in the Word. The Bible has such life and strength for someone who needs confidence. God did not see me as dumb and worthless. He created me in His image.

I continued down the path of self-destruction. I married my boyfriend, believing no one else would want me. I rationalized that since he was a pastor, things would get better, and I would fix the things that were wrong with me. I was wrong. The abuse continued and so did my low self-image issues. I was a pastor's wife having to put on a façade of a wonderful life while being put down daily. Sitting on the front row at church listening to my preacher husband knowing what had been said and done to me a couple of hours before really did a number on me. I was living a Christian life, but that life was not living inside of me. I was not living that confident life that only Christ could give me. I was not living that life that would make me confident in a God who saw me as his own precious child.

I was blessed with two children who became my life. As a mom, I devoted myself to them. I felt worth as a mother that I didn't feel as a wife. My husband worked more and more away from home at our church, and I worked on becoming the best mother that I could be. The marriage could not survive as it was. One night, my husband sat me down and said he had found someone else and was leaving me and our two children. Part of me was relieved, but I was afraid of life as a single mother.

Having to provide for my children worked on my psyche. Even though I had not been the one to leave our marriage, I felt I had contributed. I shoved those feelings down where I would not have to deal with them, which is, I later learned, how I tried to cope. But it didn't work. Eventually, all feelings will have to be dealt with.

So we set about in the next chapter of our lives. God was still with us. He never left. God enabled me to get back into the teaching field. We were on the path to recovery. I was attending a church in the area when I met my second husband. He appeared to be a man of God and loved me and my children. We married, and I thought we were very happy. But it was all a fantasy. My second husband's secret would destroy us. He was arrested and because of the severity of the crime, I had to protect my children and seek a divorce. My children had been affected by his actions, causing the guilt I had buried to raise its ugly head. Negative thoughts took over. I told myself, "You are a loser; you couldn't even see what was happening in your own home. You will lose your children, and they will never recover and will never forgive you." Because I had not learned to turn off the negative voices and listen to my Jesus's words of freedom, I felt even worse about myself. But Jesus was patiently waiting. We had found a wonderful church, and it was there that I finally learned some difficult lessons. First was the importance of praise. I immersed myself in songs that were encouraging and words that fed my soul. I learned to see myself as God sees me. God sees me as His precious jewel. He sees me as royalty. I can never do anything or endure any situation that would take me out of God's hand. Secondly, I remained in the church because there, I gained my strength. I also had to have my children at church, because they needed to hear from God just as much as I did. Third, I read the Bible and learned to speak verses over my life. I believe before I was born, God knew the plan for me and my children. He patiently waited, and I know beyond a shadow of a doubt that God was with us through everything we had to endure. Lastly, I taught my children how to endure. We had setbacks, but God always saw us through. And each time, I talked to my children about what God had done. My children were encouraged by church and their youth groups.

Things did not get better overnight. I went through bankruptcy, I was sued by a landlord, and I lost more than one job. But my outlook was so different. Instead of blaming myself and indulging in negative self-talk, I thought, "Okay, God, I know we can handle this together."

While I haven't always known it, I know now that like Queen Esther, I was created for such a time as this. I am sharing my story so that you can be encouraged. Whatever you are going through, you can do it, but only with God's help. When my world was crashing, I did not want to tell God that He was great and perfect in all His ways. But I did it anyway. Find a good church to attend. Do not be afraid to share with someone what you are going through. Keep your children involved and tell them of the great things God is doing for you.

This is my story, but it is not my life.

ESTHER, GAINESVILLE, GA

I was born in New Orleans, Louisiana, to an unmarried college student. My mom met my dad, a musician and barkeeper at the time, while visiting my maternal grandmother's workplace. He was quite the schmoozer who could talk with anyone about anything. My father was also a ladies' man, with a keen eye for younger ladies like my mom, who was 14 years his junior. One thing led to another for them, but by the time I was born, my father was no longer in the picture. Did he realize the foundation that he was laying for me?

With my biological father gone, mom in college and a working grandmother, someone had to care for me. So my family decided it would be best for me to live with my great-grandparents in Foxworth, Mississippi. The 60-somethings, with the help of my teenage aunt, were taking care of a newborn. I still have a faint memory of crawling above my paw-paw's head while he and my maw-maw lay in bed talking. I remember him holding me in his arms while sitting in the front porch swing as it swayed back and forth. I recall being loved. Did my paw-paw realize the foundation that he was laying for me? He passed away a few days before my first birthday.

My mam-maw and aunt, left to care for a one-year-old who was walking and trying to trying to talk, nurtured my inquisitive nature through hands-on, tactical learning like playing with blocks and working in the garden. They taught me to recognize and say the alphabet, to count, and how to write my name. When I was a toddler, my great-grandmother taught me to recite Psalms 23 and other bible verses. It brought her great pleasure that I was able to memorize scripture and reiterate it upon command. "The Lord is my Shepard, I shall not want" still resonates in my heart and my spirit. Did my mam-maw realize the foundation she was laying for me? Did my aunt, who endured my unending efforts to court the young men who came to see her, realize her impact on my life?

When it was time for me to go to kindergarten, I moved back to New Orleans to live with my mother, stepfather, and baby sister. My memories of spending time with my immediate family prior this time of my life are vague. I recall a baby bed with a mobile and my sister as an infant, but I have no true memories of being engaged in family life. Living in the city was a stark contrast to living on our family land in Mississippi. New Orleans was urban landscape. We lived in a working-class neighborhood not far from a major highway and railroad tracks. How I relished hearing the sound of the train rolling along the tracks; however, I did not enjoy the frequent sounds of rage and conflict between my mom and stepfather. I especially disliked the physical altercations that sometimes resulted. This went on for years, from one residence to another, sometimes even in the presence of others. Once during a 137-mile drive from Crosby, Mississippi, back home, an argument arose. In the dusk of the evening, my stepfather stopped the car, got out, pulled my mom out of the car and struck her. Not knowing where we were or what would happen to us, my sister and I held on to each other. Did my parents know the foundation they were laying for us?

But through it all, we were in church every Sunday. My mother sang in the choir, and my stepfather became a minister. My sister and I sang in the children's choir, participated in Sunday School and other church activities. Still, we continued to witness fussing, fighting, and adultery at home. It seemed commonplace for men to have extramarital affairs and display inappropriate behavior towards women, even in the church. Our pastor once told me he advocated young women taking birth control and the use of condoms. I did not initially view this statement as too outrageous or even offensive, as I had similar views. But when he suggested we should have lunch or dinner sometime to discuss the subject further, I grew wary. Did he, a married man and pastor, not realize the impact of his words and his proposed actions?

Seven years later, not completely aware of how it happened, I was walking down the aisle to say "I do." Three years before, a handsome man with loads of swagger moved next door to my roommate and me. I wanted to meet him, so I did. I learned he had just moved to Atlanta from Buffalo, New York. He was eight years older than me, previously served in the Navy, was single, and had a 3-year old son. We talked a few times, went to dinner, to the movies. We were dating, but my distrust of men eventually became a problem.

I had witnessed my stepfather's and the pastor's behavior toward women. I was distrustful and could read the signs of infidelity. "You've been gone way too long. Where have you been?" I would demand. I didn't recognize the impact the actions of others had on my life and in my relationship. I definitely didn't understand the impact of my words.

Despite all the accusations and doubt, we moved in together. It troubled my spirit to live in sin, but I rationalized that others in my family were doing it, too. I was lying to myself. I would stay on my side of the bed, so he couldn't touch me in any way. The arguments started again, and our trust level plummeted. He began checking my cell phone, and I began staying at work later. We slept in separate bedrooms. Yet we still went to church on Sundays and professed our love for God and each other. What were we doing?

My heart eventually softened, and I began to show love and compassion toward my mate. He was receptive; although I had not been as responsive to his efforts to woo me. I recognized he was a good man, but there was something there that gave me angst, though I tried to ignore it and focus on the good.

During dinner at our favorite restaurant, he proposed. After our meal, dessert arrived. When I lifted my spoon, dangling from it was an engagement ring. My future husband dropped to one knee and asked me to marry him. Through tears of joy (and confusion), I agreed to be his wife. We were married in July of the following year.

We weren't ready for marriage and a couple of weeks after taking our vows, the arguments started again. Four weeks after being married, we found out that we were expecting. I was surprised by my husband's lack of enthusiasm at the news. But I never expected him to leave me two weeks later after learning of the pregnancy.

I did not want to raise a child alone, so I tried to make things right between us. We sought pastoral counseling, I begged, I pleaded, I offered many compromises – all to no avail. Our son was born exactly nine months from the date we married. I worried about how I would care for him. But from the moment I first held him in my arms, I knew I would love him forever, and that I wanted him to know that he was loved.

For months after the birth of our son, we talked about getting back together – to make our family whole, but it never came to fruition. Stressed and ashamed, I moved back to New Orleans with my 10-month-old son. I needed the support of my family. I wanted to feel loved and treasured. So many days and nights I cried out to God seeking peace, asking Him why I had to go through this agony. As a child, I had witnessed my mom go through similar anguish and frustration. Now, she sat in her chair every night reading the Word and seeking to better understand God's will for her life. Was she perfect in her walk? No, but she was seeking. There was something in her that needed more of Him. Her life had been impacted by her trust in God and His love for her. I needed more of Him. Through the pain, I learned to truly trust in the Lord with all of my heart and to not lean on my own understanding. I learned to acknowledge Him and to allow Him to direct my path. I follow God's lead, which has led to increased faith and complete trust in Him.

Recently, my faith was again tested. In June of 2015, a CAT scan revealed that the frontal lobe of my brain had partially sunken into my sinus cavity. In addition to dealing with my best friend's mom being murdered, my grandmother being admitted to hospice, and my son going away for his first year of college, I had to have brain surgery. Worry and stress would accomplish nothing, so I leaned on God for my strength. He is my refuge. When my son was asked how he was dealing with my impending surgery, he responded, "It's all in God's control." I made it through surgery without incident. After recuperating at home for six weeks with the loving support of family and friends, I was able to return to work with little impact on my performance. A post-operative MRI confirmed the surgery's success. Praise be to God!

The words we say and the actions we take impact not only our life, but the lives of others. You never know who is watching you, who is listening to you. Ask God to order your steps – to let the words of your mouth and the meditation of your heart be acceptable in His sight. Neither my faith nor my walk have not been perfect, but my God is perfect and ever faithful. This profession is my legacy.

This is my story, but it is not my life.

MONICA, TUCKER, GA

I am the eldest of ten children. I come from a long line of strong, independent women. I was raised in a Christian home by a single mom who worked really hard to provide what we needed and some of what we wanted. My mom gave birth to me when she was 15 years old. My father was not in my life during my childhood, and I didn't meet him face-to-face until I turned 35 years old. My mom and my grandma told me the story of my conception and how my dad denied I was his. When I was 6 years old, I got all As on my report card and wanted my dad to know about it. Perhaps, then, he would want me. I had heard my mom and grandma talk about him hanging out around the corner from our house in a bar. So, wearing ruffled socks, a pretty dress and bows in my hair, I walked to the bar and tried to push the big black door open. It was too heavy, but a man was coming out, and I walked in. It was kind of dark and smoky. I could see the legs of the silver barstools and the black floor. A man asked me, "Baby, what are you doing in here?" I replied, "Looking for my daddy."

"What's your daddy name?"

"Wilbert Powers."

"He's not here," he said. Something in me broke. I cried all the way home and never said a word about that day until I became an adult. Rejection, abandonment, and an orphan spirit shaped the woman I became. I had daddy issues.

My grandma was a great influence in my life growing up. We talked about everything, especially men and how to handle them. She used to say, "A woman can get any man to do anything she wants. It's all about how she uses her bait." She told me to never be with a man that doesn't work harder than me. Not every man will have money, but he must have money's worth, meaning he needs to know how to fix something or build something or know someone who does. She also taught me not to count on a man to do anything for me. She valued a woman's ability to make things happen for herself. "A man," she always said, "will do whatever it takes to catch the woman that he wants, and a woman will let herself be caught by the man that she wants. And in between the chasing and being caught, a lot of business gets taken care of."

By the time I got married at 24, these truths were deeply embedded in my spirit. I quickly found out that a marriage certificate does not make a marriage. I had no clue of what I was doing. The only examples I had of marriage were not good. My grandmother's husband left her with ten children, a bag of beans in the cupboard, and eight cents on the mantel. My mother's husband was a golf caddy, and five months into the marriage he started traveling all over the United States. When he managed to make it home, he saw his other women, too, and he left my mom pregnant. After ten years, she divorced him.

My heart didn't feel worthy of love, and I wouldn't let my husband close enough to hurt me. I was hardened, and I always had a plan to take care of me. But God had a better plan. He sent me a man that was everything that I wasn't and needed. He was full of joy, happy, and loved me to pieces. It took me years to become comfortable with his displays of affection that didn't have to do with sex, because I had no clue what true intimacy was. I was irritated when he wanted to hold my hand or sit close to me while we watched television. Later, I understood God was using my husband to father me.

The first seven years of our marriage were intense. Whenever I couldn't have my way, I wanted a divorce and threatened to leave him before he left me. Eventually things began to settle down with us, and we found our rhythm. Seeking a fresh start away from our families, we sold our furniture, gave away most of our possessions, left Louisiana and joined my husband's brother in Atlanta on New Year's Day, 1987. Things didn't exactly go exactly as planned. In fact, they got a whole lot worse before they got better. We were actually homeless for a short time, staying in our car. It was a great motivator to reconnect with God in a way that I had never done before. It took a few months, but God's favor prevailed.

We found jobs and a place to live. We found a church home that we loved and eventually made some great relationships. The more time we spent with our new friends, the more discontented I became with my station in life. From the outside looking in, they had it all. I didn't know this at the time, but I began working overtime to erase the past that I was ashamed of and create a new one I thought would be acceptable to people I really didn't know.

I became very skilled at the art of presentation: clothes, shoes, jewelry etc. I kept talking to my husband about working together to reach a common goal, but it seemed to me he had no ambition, and I told him so every chance I got. I was out of control. During one of our many heated arguments, I said to him, "You are not my dream husband. He would be six feet tall and a business man."

I had all of the answers. I worked two jobs and did as much overtime as they would allow me to do. While I was working like a Hebrew slave to keep up with the Joneses, I was destroying my marriage. My husband of eight years was having an affair and was planning on leaving me for the other woman. The pain of that betrayal nearly destroyed me. It completely transformed me into an angry, bitter woman who made his life a living hell for a long time. I refused to listen to anything he had to say. And I was too pissed off to pray.

But our God is so faithful and knows what we need before we ask. Sitting there alone in my room, I asked, "Lord, how did we end up here? God revealed some hard truths to me: He commanded women to respect their husbands and husbands to love their wives. My husband had loved me, but I hadn't respected him.

God showed me how wounds that have not been healed will continue to show up and have a negative impact on your life. Healing is a journey, and it is also a choice. At some point, my authentic-self had to be good enough. Through much prayer and counseling, God connected us to couples who taught me how to be a Godly wife and helped to heal my broken pieces. Our marriage became better than it was before. God used the life I was so desperately trying to erase to heal me and the lives of countless women through me. The people I thought I needed to change myself for already loved me for me and recognized that I had the gift of counseling in me long before I did.

Now happily married for 35 years, we are growing. God is blessing me to make a living by healing the lives of hurt and broken women. God made a miracle out of my mess, and He can do the same for you.

This is my story, but it is not my life.

GAYLE, BATON ROUGE, LA

I found myself asking the same questions over and over again. Did I make the right choice when I decided to end my marriage after five years? Did I give it enough time? Did I try hard enough to keep it together? What about our daughter?

When we first got married, he would pray every morning in the shower, and we would attend church together. After three years, I noticed he no longer prayed, and we no longer attended church together. My first mistake was never addressing the situation.

I called my mother and told her what was going on and how I was feeling. My mother and father have been married for more than 56 years and still enjoy each other's company. My parents had their share of arguments, but hours after my parent's argument, they would be laughing and talking with each other once again. And I had my three sisters and my brother to attach to. My child had no one.

I wanted him gone. I had to be passive when we were arguing because my child looked scared and confused. I begged him not to argue in front of our daughter, but my requests seemed to make him shout louder. I tried to defuse the situation to protect our daughter, but my husband took my silence as a weakness. Eventually, I would find the right time to take him down.

My conversations with my mother didn't go the way I had hoped it would. She was old school and thought I should stay and work it out, warning me of other women's willingness to step right on in. She was worried about what people might say or think. I didn't necessarily agree, but after several conversations with my mother, I made the agonizing decision to stay and try to figure it out.

I asked my husband to go to church with me, implored him to talk to me, and told him I loved him. It was a lie. I didn't love him anymore. I didn't want to make it work; I wanted him gone, but I was trying to save face for my mother and keep a father in the household for my child.

Then it hit me. Maybe he didn't love me either. A conversation with him revealed the love was gone, but he wasn't going anywhere.

Another year passed, and things got worse. One night, I dreamed a small, dark troll-like creature was trying to get me. I kept saying, "I rebuke you in the name of Jesus." It jumped off me and ran upstairs into my child's room. I panicked, tossing and turning, trying to wake up so I could get to my child, but I could not move. I repeated, "I rebuke you in the name of Jesus. In the name of Jesus, I rebuke you. I rebuke you from my child." The troll jumped off her and ran into my bedroom where my husband was sleeping. The door closed. I said nothing.

I went into my daughter's room, picking her up to take her downstairs with me. Again, I saw the door to my bedroom closed and did nothing. I didn't care what happened to him. What a profound dream.

I knew it was time for me to move on. I sent my child away for the summer, so I could put my plan in motion to get rid of this man once and for all. I yelled at him and wailed, trying to provoke him, but he said and did nothing.

I couldn't take it anymore. One Saturday afternoon, I challenged him to a fist fight. I said, "Your daughter isn't here now and you can yell as loud as you want, but I'm ready to whip your ass." He looked scared and shocked.

I punched at him; I was trying to hit him in that big mouth. He came back at me, but missed. We tussled for a while. I was really giving him a run for his money. He was able to get a punch in and hit me in the lip. I lost all reason. We ended on the bed. He was trying to take my ring off my finger. I yelled, "You're gonna have to cut this finger off."

I was tired, so I fell off the bed, pretending to have hurt my back. He apologized and proclaimed his love for me. I had no intention of calling 911, but the threat got him to leave the house – exactly what I wanted.

When I told my daughter her father was gone, she took it really hard. And when I told my mother about how bad things had gotten, she had my back.

We didn't divorce right away, but he pulled away from our daughter and wasn't helping out financially. I hired an attorney and filed for child support. Our divorce became final, and my ex-husband cut ties with our child. But I made her feel special, and she never asked questions.

Life was good until I got laid off from my job and we began to have financial difficulties. That's when I started to question whether I made the right decision. My child was listening to her father bash me and began to blame me for everything that was wrong. I was hurt because I was struggling to make ends meet and protecting her from the pain and suffering I was going through. I had promised myself I would not confuse her by bashing him and telling her the real truth.

I focused on her following the divorce, and in five years, I had not dated. But it was time. Unfortunately, the men I met were married seeking side chicks or single liars. I wondered, Why are all the cheaters and liars approaching me? Are there any decent men in this entire state?

I couldn't focus on men while I was losing my daughter. We were having some bad days. A therapist was in order. To my surprise, though, the therapist said my daughter was fine. She was concerned about me based on some things my daughter had told her.

My child told the therapist I was always lying in bed watching TV and when I was up, I moved like a turtle.

I was hurt and shocked. I had been trying to shield my daughter from our financial situation, but she saw my depression. With the therapist's guidance, I recovered very quickly, and both of us continued therapy. I thank God for my therapist and my daughter.

I have been in bondage since I allowed the troll into my house, and the times I didn't pray him off my husband. I knew it was wrong and I have asked for forgiveness from the Lord. Now I am working to forgive myself.

This is my story, but it is not my life.

SHARON, CHARLOTTE, NC

It was a typical Sunday morning. At church, it was a time of gladness, greeting each other as we began another week in our place of worship. I could hear the sound of musical notes from within the sanctuary signaling it was time to be seated. Moving toward the entrance, I noticed several women I didn't recognize lingering outside as if waiting for someone. I would have welcomed them had I not heard their comments. Their words felt like the stings of angry hornets. One said, "There she is." Then, she added, in a tone sounding like disbelief, "She's pretty!"

I thought, "Who are they talking about?" When I turned to get a closer look at them, they walked away. It was then that I intuitively knew these were the women from my husband's office – the women with whom he had affairs. These were the women who had filed the human resources complaints against him. Had they come just to see what I looked like? I was humiliated and stunned!

At the time, I wasn't aware they had previously brought their complaints to our pastor. My husband was a deacon. I don't know how much time lapsed between the conversation with our pastor and hornet Sunday, but I know it was only when my husband became convinced they would contact me directly that he told me everything. I was hurt and angry, but not surprised. There had been red flags of infidelity. Bills arriving for unrecognized purchases, installation of a second phone line in an unfinished basement, a woman answering his hotel room phone after midnight while he was away on a business trip. Soon he lost his job and moved to another state. After a period of separation, we divorced.

I was a respected leader for 18 years in that church. Then, the lies of my husband sent my life into a tailspin from which it took years to recover. He assassinated my character with our pastor, and by the time I found out, the damage was done. He implied I had a disreputable background. I couldn't believe I was never told or given the chance to substantiate the allegations. Adding insult to injury were a few crafty women who mounted a malicious harassment campaign against me. At first, I didn't recognize what was happening. When I did, it was clear that I was on the front line of spiritual warfare. I was hit from all sides by weapons of intimidation and manipulation. I thought I might have been having a breakdown. Each day was like walking through a dense fog into a sunny clearing and back again. I could see some things clearly while others were a confusing blur of unknowns. My body was showing signs of stress; I was exhausted and losing weight. My joy was not gone but strained. When I felt the fog wasn't lifting on its own, I scheduled an appointment with my doctor.

I continued to study God's word and pray for guidance. One evening as I was reading the Book of Job, I wrote in my journal about how he must have felt as he endured his many losses, suffered the ridicule of friends and his wife. My life during the darkest days felt like I was Job. His strength, like mine, was faith in God's mercy and grace which continued to be of comfort when I was faced with things I don't fully understand. I learned through numerous battles that for those who love the Lord, there will be lost battles along the way, but eventually, the war will be won.

Dealing with long-term stress taught me a lot about myself. I was vulnerable, but strong. I was a fighter. I was willing to cry a little – just a little. It was more important for me to get up quickly to search for answers and solutions and to find insights I either didn't know or had paid little attention to. I sought God in a new way as I prayed for the guidance and the understanding only He can provide.

With the help of a trusted couple that sought me out, I was able to admit to myself that I had, during my marriage, been beaten down over time with words. My abilities were devalued and my entire life was tied to one group of people and activities. My life was unbalanced; so much so that when I broke away, I stood alone. A few special angels came forward providing needed resources that made life a bit easier. For them and the time and energy they gave to help me move forward, I am grateful.

Staying for a while, I struggled with the pastor's willingness to believe and share an accusation without careful investigation. In my idealistic view, it was unthinkable. My belief compass was broken. I had seen church through rose-colored glasses, but I learned people are people, wherever they are. None are without flaws; all are in need of forgiveness.

I left the church I'd served in for many years, sold my home, cut off all contact with everyone I'd been associated with and started over. I purchased a new home in another city. It fills with the natural light each morning and remains bright all day, with a wildlife preserve just a few feet from my backdoor. I enjoy photographing the new life in a deer family each year.

I started a business, joined a local book club, and joined a new church. I had learned to diversify my relationships. I began volunteering in the community and serving in the missions ministry at my new church. I became active in street ministry for the homeless and have served on short-term mission trips in the US as well as in three international countries.

I prayed for freedom to live, work, have a variety of friend groups, and serve God according to my spiritual as well as natural gifts and abilities. God answered my prayers and brought me to fullness of life.

I became an improved version of my old self. I began to live my life more meaningfully. My spirituality has been strengthened by choosing to be led by the Holy Spirit in all things. I discovered my gifts and continue to grow in Christian education and beneficial things that pique my interest.

This is my story, but it is not my life.

OPHELIA, MARION, VIRGINIA

I got married at the age of 18, because I was pregnant. My mom told me I didn't have to get married, but in my ninth month, I was standing at the altar saying "I do." My husband was physically abusive, even before we got married. When we met, I was 14, and he was 17 and he was very manipulative. I stayed with him, because I was afraid he would carry out his threats to harm my family if I spoke of the abuse.

Two months after my son was born, my husband was incarcerated for armed robbery. He came from a well-to-do family, with whom I continued to live after he was arrested, and even though I knew his father's abuse contributed to his rebelliousness, I was relieved and felt free when he got locked up. I came to realize that my low expectations were tied to my low self-esteem, triggered by sexual abuse at the hands of my parents' boarder when I was 5 years old.

I was determined my son would not turn out like his father. To begin making a better life for the both of us, I went to school to become a legal secretary and eventually studied to be a paralegal.

I moved out of their house. I worked two jobs, went to school in the evening, and leaned heavily on my parents to pick up the slack to raise my son. I found out later that my strict parents were giving my son free reign. He was being influenced by his older cousins and getting into trouble.

My mom had kidney disease and had to be on dialysis. My son, then 13, was misbehaving. I had a decision to make.

In 1986, I was working as a legal assistant for SEPTA, Philadelphia's mass transit authority, when one of my best friends moved to Atlanta. She kept trying to get me to relocate, raving about the weather. It was hard to believe. I was trudging through 11 inches of snow, while she wore shorts in November.

She eventually convinced me to visit, and as soon as I arrived in the airport, I said "I'm moving!" I knew in my heart it was the move for me.

I broke the news to my mom, and although I saw the sadness and disbelief in her eyes, I knew I couldn't save my both mother and my son. I chose to move to Atlanta for my son and, unfortunately, I lost both of them.

My son prospered in Atlanta from ages 13 to 16, but good times didn't last. He started hanging out with the wrong crowd and making horrible choices. I lost my mom to her illness and my only child to the penal system.

After my only child called to tell me he was on the run for murder, I collapsed on the floor and began rocking back and forth in a ball, crying out to God. I had no family in Georgia, and I felt more alone than I had ever felt. Although my son did not pull the trigger, he was sentenced to 40 years without the possibility of parole.

I did not know the Lord was on His way to save me. I was working at a large corporation, and on this particular day, there was a temp who happened to be a minister working in the mailroom. While I was collecting the mail for my office, I heard the gospel music she was playing. When I broke down in tears, she embraced and comforted me. She asked me if I would receive Jesus in my life. I agreed and was baptized on Sunday in June of 1995. My life started changing the day I decided to release my son to God and attend church. Unfortunately, the anguish, pain, and disappointment, coupled with guilt over my son's incarceration, had taken a toll on my health. In 1996, I was diagnosed with Crohn's Disease.

Crohn's Disease is an ongoing disorder that is associated with inflammation of the gastrointestinal (GI) tract. It can affect any area of the GI tract, typically the end of the small bowel and the beginning of the large intestine, causing pain and diarrhea. As a result of this disease, I was down from 125 pounds to about 90 pounds. I was taking 21 pills per day and going into the hospital every two months to get blood transfusions for up to four hours at a time. My health was deteriorating, and my job was also at risk. I only told a few people about my disease and dared not tell my family for fear of being asked to move back to Philadelphia. Fortunately, I did not lose my job then, but I continued to suffer in silence for several years. It wasn't until I went home for a visit and my family saw how thin, tired, and listless I had become that I confessed.

My life consisted of doctors' visits, medicine, and work. A good friend was having a birthday party and begged me to attend, even though she knew how ill I was. I relented, planning to go to the party, listen to the live band for a little while, then head back home. I was sitting at a table when my eyes locked with one of the musicians in the band. It was an instant attraction and suddenly my heart started to feel something I hadn't felt in a long time.

After the event, he walked me to my car, and we exchanged numbers. I refused to go on a date with him because of a bad date experience several weeks prior. After eating, I had excused myself from the table three times, and my date accused me of talking to another guy secretly on my cell phone. I was visibly upset and confessed my disease. Although he was apologetic, I never went out with him again. I couldn't risk that humiliation again.

I avoided my new friend for three weeks before finally agreeing to go out with him. After excusing myself several times to go to the bathroom, he asked if I was okay. I broke down in tears and told him about my Crohn's Disease. My date looked at me and asked, "Is that all?" Then, he took my hands and declared that by God's stripes, I was healed.

I granted him permission to come to my house. He went through my refrigerator and cabinets and tossed everything into the trash. My head told me to call the cops, but my heart stopped me. This guy not only tossed out all my bad food, but he took me shopping to replenish my refrigerator and cabinets with healthy foods. Along with prayer, supplements, faith and, a changed diet, I was free of Crohn's Disease in a matter of three months. That man, a Christian and nutritionist, became my husband.

Together, we formed a health ministry and were able to help many people regain their health. After being married for about eight years, he stopped going to church and left me for another woman. I hugged him, thanked him, and wished him well. Was I hurt? Absolutely! But this man, chosen by God, gave me my life back, and I was grateful.

I was going through a divorce, when I was one of 500 people laid off by my company. My father was losing his battle with heart disease, and my brother was dealing with liver disease. When my husband left, we were two months behind with our mortgage. Creditors were calling non-stop. But God!

I was always interested in aviation, so when I found out my company had invited the Tuskegee Airmen to show artifacts and take pictures, I was ecstatic! I met a pilot that day and, instead of taking pictures and talking about the Tuskegee Airmen, he talked to me about coffee, a beverage I did not enjoy. He told me about the primary herb infused in these products. As a leader of a health ministry, that definitely got my attention. I started passing out coffee and tea samples, and my boss came back to my desk three times asking for more coffee.

I knew I was on to something. I took my last $1,500 in savings and invested in Organo Gold in 2010. Within a year, I acquired loads of customers and several business partners. I had found another source of income without getting a traditional second job.

I had lost my job, my dad, and my brother. I was desperate to keep my house and find another job, but I didn't realize my age would make it challenging to find work. I was forced to work my coffee business full-time, while attemping to generate additional income.

The year 2015 gave me time to go within and connect with God on an amazing level. I learned to rely on Him to take care of me. Are things perfect? No, but I have trust and peace that surpasses all understanding. I'm still growing my business, and I am totally trusting God to pour out blessings I won't have enough room to receive.

This is my story, but it is not my life.

KAREN, PHILADELPHIA, PA

On December 31, 2012, I was sitting in the back row of my church during watch night service. I was at my lowest point. My father-in-law had recently passed away from brain cancer and a month later, I decided to separate from my husband. At the time, I was living almost three hours away from my family in a small rural town. I absolutely despised it. I didn't know if it was the town I couldn't stand, or if it was the memories I detested. I had graduated from college in 2010 and still had not found a decent paying job. The country was coming out of the Recession, but it seemed as if it wasn't recovering fast enough to compensate for all I had lost. All of my sacrifices felt as if they were in vain. The struggle to graduate was hard enough. My senior year, I had gotten married, and soon thereafter, my son was conceived. Although we were married, the pregnancy was unplanned. The pressure from school, working two low wage jobs and trying to make ends meet was very stressful. I had no idea how I was going to feed and provide for this little human being that God was putting me in charge of. I became depressed because I did not have a support system. I sacrificed staying in that small town to graduate from school. I went to all but one of my obstetrician appointments alone. I did not have anyone there to hold my hand or guide me through it. I was so sad and depressed while I was pregnant, I prayed every night for the Lord to bless my son with a happy spirit. I did not want my stress to affect him chemically.

The bigger my belly grew, the more afraid my husband became. Instead of maturing, he regressed. He became less responsible and more detached. When I gave birth to my son, my whole life changed. I didn't feel the overwhelming joy most mothers feel. I thought something was possibly wrong with me. I was terrified, but I fought through that feeling to do whatever was best for my son. I knew I was suffering from postpartum depression, but I could not let that stop me. By the grace of God, my son was born with the most beautiful spirit! He was such a happy and loving baby. He was my light in my dark moment. God used him to help keep me focused.

I was down to my last few credit hours in school, and I was determined to finish. I was told I wasn't going to be able to graduate, and that only forced me to push harder. My last semester of school, I took my son to daycare, went to my internship, went to classes, went to work at night, tried to be a good mother to my son, and started all over the next day. I have no idea how I endured physically, except God stepped in. During that semester, I was also homeless. My husband and I were supposed to move into a rental house, but the day we were moving out of our apartment, the new property manager told us we could not move in. For more than a week, my husband stayed with his best friend. My son and I stayed with a coworker's parents, and I prayed we were not being a burden. My husband was perfectly fine with his family staying with people we barely knew, while he was hanging out with friends. He partied, while I managed my typical routine and slept in a stranger's house with my teething seven month old son. It was rough, but it was a sacrifice I was willing to make. When we were finally able to move into our house, my routine stayed the same. The load was almost too heavy to bear, but God provided me with the strength to make it across the finish line.

After graduation, I continued to fight depression. I was so miserable living in that city. I wanted to move, but my husband insisted we stay. I stayed in that city, miserable, for two years for him. When I finally could not take it anymore, I told him I would move on my own with our son. He was enraged and called me selfish. He had the audacity to say it with conviction – as if I had not sacrificed my happiness for two years waiting for him…waiting for him to get the promotion he never got…waiting for him to lead our family which, in reality, he was completely incapable of doing, because he was not putting God first. The entire time I was waiting, I was dying inside, committing spiritual suicide. I longed for a church home and tried to attend different services around the small city. No place agreed with my spirit like my home church. Each time I returned, disappointed after a service, my husband made very discouraging remarks. He questioned why I was trying so hard to find a place to worship. I was looking for that spiritual connection and couldn't find it. I didn't see God in my husband or any of his actions. I found it very hard to love a man I couldn't see God in.

I became very cold and distant as a form of protection for myself; or so I thought. God was not in my marriage, but God was in me. I had so much talent, and it was being wasted. I knew I could no longer grow where I was planted. It was time to find new soil. When I separated from my husband, I had no idea what I was going to do. It was one of the hardest decisions I ever made that I do not regret. This move was completely about trusting in God and watching Him work. Once I took that step out on faith, He began to lay the stepping stones for me to cross. I was able to transfer my job and only four weeks later found new employment that paid more. Although I was living with my parents, I always had the mindset to be on my own.

When I stopped being his emotional punching bag, he was faced with seeing himself for what he truly was…a bully. He always suspected me of cheating and would go through my phone while I was sleeping. He confessed he never found anything. I always told him if I ever left him, it would be for myself and no one else. In all honesty, I did leave him for someone; I left him to be closer to Jesus. The whole time I was lost, I always knew God was waiting and watching over me. In an extremely low moment, I wanted to drive off of a bridge into traffic. In that moment, God spoke to me and told me to go home. In a flash, I realized how selfish that would have been of me. Who would have taken care of my son? Who would have nurtured him and molded him as only a mother can? At that moment, I realized I would not let anyone come between me and God, because the closer I am to God, the better mother, and person, I am.

While I was seeking God's face I began to read my Bible more. There was something that needed to drastically change in my life. I signed up for a total transformative process through my church led by my pastor. During this 40-day process, God spoke to me as He has never spoken to me before. By forgiving people for what they had done to me and forgiving myself for the things I allowed in my life, I felt lighter, freer. I actually began to glow! Midway through the process, I was in a very bad car accident. I was driving to work and another SUV T-boned my vehicle on the driver's side. My car flipped six or seven times. The car was destroyed, and pieces of debris were scattered all across the intersection.

While my car was flipping in the air, I heard nothing but silence and calmness. After I landed and realized I was still in one piece, I felt an overwhelming joy! The devil tried to take my life, but God said no!

As I sat in my car waiting to be freed from the mangled cage, God continued to speak to me. He continued to tell me that everything would be okay and that He had everything under control. After hearing His voice, I was wheeled away in an ambulance. Eight hours later, I was released from the hospital with nothing but bruises. At that moment, I realized there was a calling on my life that I had to fulfill.

When I went to my chiropractor to have my spine examined for severe neck pain, he looked at me as if I was a medical miracle. He told me that if my skull had been shifted to the right any further, I would have been paralyzed or dead. I didn't tell the doctor was that while I was flipping in the air, the Holy Spirit told me to hold my head.

That was nearly two years ago, and I am still growing with God. He has blessed me with a better paying job with great benefits and my own place to live with my son. God has greater plans in store for me, and I am excited to see what is next. I know as long as I keep my eyes focused on God and share my story with the world, He will continue to pour out such blessings I will not have room enough to receive. And I will continue to give Him all the glory and praise!

This is my story, but it is not my life.

CAMILE, MARIETTA, GA

DEATH

I remember singing *Amazing Grace* in church every time someone joined the church or whenever anyone made a public confession of faith. My Mom loved singing it; she sang in the choir. A smile lit up her face as she sang it loud and joyfully. My grandmothers loved the song, too. I remember the last birthday weekend I spent with both of them. My brother played it as we gathered round the piano. I still remember that beautiful evening.

I was blessed with strong women in my young life. My maternal grand-mother, My Lady, I called her, walked with a cane due to rickets as a child, an affliction doctors said would cause her to die young and never bear children. She proved them wrong, though, living to be 80 years old. She had five children, survived two miscarriages and lived a hard life, loving those children through extreme poverty while married to their mean, abusive father. After his death, she moved to a house on our block and stayed with us every day while my parents worked. She taught me a great deal about unconditional love, forgiveness, family, faith and devotion. My dad's mom, my MaMaw, her beautiful blue eyes sparkling full of life and love, was also actively involved in my life growing up. She was a spitfire. Many said my personality is most like hers – super sweet when all is well, but quite feisty when crossed. She was my cheerleader and always told me to stand my ground. She loved her family, her church community, and her friends with passion, and would do anything to help them. She taught me about loyalty, sacrifice, and the importance of helping others. She also taught me to believe in myself, be independent, and `never to be afraid to use my voice. I also had many years with her mother, my great-grandmother, Granny, as everyone called her. She was part Native-American, with pioneer courage and strength. Born a sharecropper's daughter, her life was hard, and she taught me to expect life to be hard and know how to handle the curve-balls life would throw at me. She also taught me how to pray every night and count my blessings as they came along. And there was my mom. She was grace personified, so consistent, stable, strong, and faithful. She loved to sing, dance, and help people. She loved her family, and her faith was strong. These ladies helped me become the woman I am, establish the foundation of my faith, and taught me the true essence of love, grace, and forgiveness.

Those women are long gone from this world, but I still know the words to that song and feel their presence in my life. My Granny died several years before my kids were born, even before I got married, while I was away at law school, and I was not able to go home for the funeral. The separation from my family during the grief was hard, but I leaned on the strength those women had taught me and thanked God for the many years I had with her.

A few years after my Granny died, after my marriage and the birth of my first-born, I was sitting at my make-up table one morning getting ready for work when a voice in my head told me to go home for my grandmothers' birthdays on November 5 and November 8, respectively. Normally, I wouldn't have gone home for their birthdays, because with a trip planned for Thanksgiving, we couldn't afford the extra expense, but the voice in my head was quite insistent. I thank God for that voice in my head and for making me listen. It was the last birthday either grandmother would celebrate. MaMaw died three weeks later, suddenly and unexpectedly, the night before Thanksgiving – the day after my husband and I arrived back home with our 16-month old daughter. The shock and devastation at the holiday was very difficult to take.

A year later, my other beloved Grandma died three days before Christmas. Her health had declined so much by her birthday the month before, she was un-aware and unable to celebrate. The voice God put in my head the year before led me home to spend that last precious birthday weekend with them. I had listened, and my faith rewarded me with beautiful memories of their celebration and their happy surprise at my coming home. I will cherish those memories a lifetime.

When my children were little, I sang to them every night when I tucked them in their beds. *Amazing Grace* was always one of the songs I sang. The lyrics brought me comfort and reminded me of my grandmothers and easier times. I told them how we sang it in my grandmother's church and my church, how much my mom, their Mimmi, loved it, and how happy she looked in the choir when she sang it.

A few years ago, we lost my mom to a severe anoxic brain injury that left her in a minimally conscious state – unable to communicate and control her emotions, bodily functions and thoughts. The pain of that year was devastating, depleting and heartbreaking. The hole her death left in our hearts was indescrib-ably large. I could no longer sing to my kids at night when I tucked them in.

At church when the band played a rendition of *Amazing Grace*, I was reduced to tears, nearly hyperventilating, because all I could picture was my mom's face when she sang it so joyfully in our home church choir. The pain of that memory was just too much to bear, given the last year of her life when the only sounds she could make were loud screams, tearful shrieks, desperate cries, and heart-wrenching groans. It was as if a light had gone out of the world.

One day, as we drove, Elvis was playing from my iPod through the car stereo. Before I realized what album was playing, Elvis began to sing *Amazing Grace*. My girls immediately recognized the song.

My oldest said, "Hey! That's the song Mommy used to sing to us when she tucked us in at night."

My middle one said, "Yes, I remember that song. I always liked that song. Mimmi liked that song, too."

Then my son chimed in, "I don't remember Mommy ever singing that song." A chill ran through me. My son couldn't remember it, because he was so young when Mom died, when I quit singing to them. Mom's last year of life and her death stopped me from singing her favorite gospel song. I let that thought sink into my brain. I knew I did not want that statement to be my son's story. I did not want it to be my daughters' stories. I did not want their stories to be that I quit singing or quit doing anything fun when they lost their Mimmi, their precious grandmother.

My kids are teenagers now, so I do not sing to them at bedtime or officially tuck them in anymore, but I do try to sing along when I hear *Amazing Grace* being played. Tears still stream down my face when I hear the song, and sometimes my voice catches, but I try to sing it for as long as I can. I still love the song, even if it is still hard to sing, and I know God understands.

A friend of mine painted an abstract portrait for my house. She writes messages in her portraits then paint over the messages, leaving the messages only partially visible. The words on the canvas were the first verse to *Amazing Grace*. Tears sprang to my eyes.

"How did you know about that song?" I asked her, trying to recall if I had mentioned anything to her of my mother's love of that song.

She paused and said, "This will sound crazy, but I've prayed about this painting, and every time I picked up a brush, I swear it was like your mom was on my shoulder telling me what to paint. She insisted it be the words to *Amazing Grace*."

My Mom and my grandmothers are all gone from my earthy presence, but God is letting me know His grace is still amazing. He knows I still need that reminder.

Amazing Grace, how sweet the sound, that saved a wretch like me, I once was lost, but now I'm found, was blind, but now I see.

This is my story, but it is not my life.

TERESA B., HOMER, LA

I am the only child of an only child of an only child. I had no one to play with. I had no real cousins, and the nearest family was on the other end of town. That left me plenty of room and time to be adventurous and mischievous. My mother divorced my father before I was 3 years old, and we lived with my grandparents, Nanny and Daddy, in a big two-story house right downtown in the upper part of East Tennessee, where mostly the whites lived. Schools were still segregated. My grandmother and mother both were teachers of one-room schools with eight grades. Coloreds, as we were referred to, could not sit at the fountain in the local drugstore while waiting for a scoop of ice cream, but they still took our money. Times were really different then. It all seems like yesterday. Looking forward, I see the price that was paid and the lessons learned. I was happy as a lark, though – no cares or worries. I thought life would be that way forever.

Growing up in an adult environment, being around grown-ups all the time, listening to gossip and old stories often made me think I was grown; however, I was always reminded children are to be seen and not heard.

Some of my fondest memories are from Sundays, because I got to see more of my friends during Sunday school and church. Sitting with my friends on the back row was our favorite thing to do. In between Sunday school and church, those of us who had money would sneak across the street to the store to buy gum, suckers, and as much candy as we could afford and our little pocketbooks would carry.

I can still hear the sounds of feet tapping as the elders at my small Presbyterian church sang hymns. Then, I didn't fully understand why they sang the same songs and some cried. But many years later – years filled with tears, heartbreak, abuse and death – I understand God's plan and expectations for my life had already been written. Could God trust me to make the journey?

I was the apple of my grandparent's eyes, and I could do no wrong. Living with them was the best. I loved them both dearly.

When the school systems became integrated, the one-room schools closed, and my mother took a job in the next town. My grandmother retired after 44 years. I drove at 13, taking my grandmother everywhere she needed to go. She became ill. We made trips to the hospital on a regular basis, and the visits became more intense. Then there was that call in the middle of the night – she had passed away ten days before my sixteenth birthday. It was my first experience with death. My world fell apart. I knew I would never get to sit in her lap or hear her say, "Everything's alright, baby." But the whole concept of death did not sink in. I watched my grandfather grieve daily, missing his best friend.

My mother thought it best that I finish at the same high school, so I lived with my grandfather. During the summer, we sat outside, and often he would talk with her. I still did not understand. Fall came, school started back, and each day he would make sure I got up to get ready for school. I got up early one morning and realized Daddy had not hollered to wake me up. I went downstairs, calling his name over and over again, but I got no answer. When I found him, he was still warm. Six days before Christmas, he had slipped away to be with my nanny. The two most important people in my life were no longer there.

I was forced to grow up really fast. My mother cried continuously over the loss of her parents, and my concerns about where I would live until graduation grew. My mother and I were like sisters and had not lived together in some time, so it was decided that I would stay in our home place with my mother's best friend until I graduated and moved away to attend college.

I didn't know the void in my life and heart was associated with death and grieving. I knew I was missing the love I had known, grown up with, and experienced. I loved God, but I began looking for love in all the wrong places and people. I made bad decisions about people and trusted all the wrong ones. I married the wrong guy for the wrong reasons, and it wasn't until after he walked out and I was alone in my sadness that I heard God say "You don't love me enough." I was shaken to the core. What could God mean? How could He question my love? But He is an all-seeing and all-knowing God, and He knew my heart.

I got deeper into the word and promised not to remarry unless God sent him with a note. Was I ever in for a surprise!

Yung and I worked for the same company, but we had never met. Then the day I was conducting a training, this man with swagger out of this world walked in the door. I knew he was the one, and so did he. Yung was my soulmate, my best friend; he stole my heart. And he wrote me a sweet note, thanking God for bringing us together, getting him on track with God, and thanking my mother for having me. It was the love I had been waiting for. We dated for two years and finally married. We took our vows seriously – to have and to hold 'til death do us part.

Life was good. Our love continued to grow. We traveled and made plans for the years to come. We laughed often about taking care of each other in our old age. Our plans were to buy a motor home and travel around the country helping people. We thought we were in good health, with a few coins in the bank. We were planning our happily ever after.

Yung always had trouble with his blood pressure and keeping his diabetes under control, but it wasn't until he had a mini-stroke, followed by a major one, that we knew how bad it was. He called me from St. Louis and asked me to dial 911. After getting the local line, some 500 miles away from where he was, I finally got the hospital near him. He was rushed there, where he received a clot buster shot. He didn't suffer any serious damage. Thanks be to God.

My husband took being the head of the household seriously, and it wasn't long before he was back at work. Unfortunately, he did not monitor his blood pressure and blood sugar while he was on the road. He ate everything that was good, but not good for him.

I traveled to Michigan to celebrate his fifty-third birthday, and our lives changed. He complained about being short of breath, blaming it on a cold or flu. We went to the local hospital to have him checked out and within hours, he was diagnosed with renal failure. Neither of us knew anything about dialysis, so all I knew to do was pray. I cried a river, and Yung assured me everything would be okay. The day the port was put into his chest, the hospital chaplain visited and prayed with us. God had sent an angel. I knew my husband would not be the same.

As we started on the transplant process, Yung had to go to dialysis three days a week for four hours. He was a trouper, despite being so physically weak. We lay in bed, and he stroked my hair and told me over and over how much he loved me. He laughed at my silly stories.

At 5:30 a.m. on January 26, he left for treatment. It was the last time we spoke. While he was waiting in the lobby for his treatment, he became unconscious. Everything that could be done was done, but he slipped from the coma to glory on February 6. My world fell apart. Yung's death was not part of the plan. Why, God? I understood we all have to die, but why my Yung – the person who held me and told me everything was going to be ok?

After the burial, I separated myself from anything that reminded me of him. I did not want to talk to anyone. I just wanted to hear his voice again. I went to prayer meetings and heard people share testimonies of healing. I left in tears, asking God why He hadn't healed my husband. On my way home, God said to me, "Even my Son had to die." I listened, I learned, I accepted, I surrendered.

I realize now it was God's plan for me to be there for Yung's journey and to minister to others about the beauty of life, living, and taking care of their health. I bought a motor home, and I travel when I can. I know what Yung and I meant to each other was real, but I have to live the life I was meant to live while he waits for me in the next room. I speak of him often, often telling how he gave so much and asked for so little.

I have learned a lot about living and life, and now I understand why the elders sang and cried. I am so thankful for God's wonderful love, grace, and mercy. When we are quiet, He can speak words of wisdom, love, and comfort. It wasn't until I told my story that I realized I had only bandaged my grief for years. Now I am free.

This is my story, but it is not my life.

MISSY POOH, KNOXVILLE, TN

My life has been shaped by the deaths of three strong forces in my life – my father, my husband and my Lord.

The death of my father.
My father died when I was a 5 years old. I have only a few faint memories of him, so what I know of him is what others have shared about him, mostly my mother, who still holds me hostage with her curiously long rants about him being a bad husband and his extramarital affairs. She was always making disparaging statements, such as "Sam never gave a damn about y'all." and "You know you probably have some other brothers or sisters out there."

I often marveled at how well she held on to her pain and memories of him. She tells these stories with such venom that most people would be shocked to know they took place more than 45 years ago. My mother wanted me to become an ally in her pain and war against this terrible man, but for as long as I can remember, I have had an inner dialogue against her rants. In my head, I asked, "If he was so bad, why did you marry him?" and "Isn't there one thing he did right?" Perhaps I would have been her ally if she had shared a more balanced view of him.

She failed to gain me as an ally, but she was successful in damaging my self-esteem. She created a terrible void with her rants, an emptiness that drove me head-on into promiscuity. I never sought therapy, but I can admit sex made me feel wanted and gave me a false sense of intimacy. It felt good for a man to compliment me on my physical appearance; the affirmation filled a need I had for male attention. But sex came with a price – unwanted pregnancies, a sexually transmitted disease, and low self-esteem. My low self-esteem made me lower my standards, though I knew I had to change my ways. I knowingly lay with a man whom I knew was both promiscuous and bi-sexual. Still in his apartment feeling like a dog, I ushered up a secret prayer to a God I wasn't sure I believed in. "Please help me."

It wasn't long thereafter that help came in the form of a minister who counseled both heterosexual and bisexual men. Eventually, he introduced me to Christ and became my husband. During the pastor's appreciation ceremony, my aunt – my father's youngest sister and only surviving sibling – presented me with a beautifully framed picture of my father. She told me she wanted me to know that my father truly loved me and was very proud of me and my sisters. I broke. At 50, I was hearing for the first time that my father loved me. It was as if God, through my aunt, wanted me to know that what I had done to myself stemmed from a lie. Later, my cousin confirmed what my aunt said. She was shocked to hear my mother's account of my dad. She offered, "Tracy, you were too young to remember, but Uncle Sam always came home from leave and got us." She continued, "He always talked about how much he loved you all and how proud he was of you."

After so much time, I didn't feel the need to confront my mother. I simply showed her the picture and told her what had been said. It was a pivotal time in our relationship. The truth had been revealed. My mother's eyes said what her mouth could not utter. She was deeply ashamed. Later, I heard her speaking to my son. She asked, "Did anyone ever tell you about your grandfather? He was very smart and strong. You would have really liked him." Priceless!!!

The death of my husband:

I met Larry at a mental health treatment facility for adolescents in Atlanta, Georgia. We were both counselors serving on an all-female unit. He and I had long discussions about life, God and religion. Although I was turned off by his brutal honesty and arrogance, I was mesmerized by his ability to articulate and explain very complicated biblical principles. Then an atheist, I was not easily swayed by religious rhetoric, so his candor and zeal made him that much more authentic to me. I questioned, he listened, and he answered. I watched him, secretly hoping he would slip up and be inappropriate with a female, but he never was. He had my attention.

Eventually, I visited Larry's church. I wanted Larry to be right. I wanted God to be real, but I needed proof. As I listened to the pastor, who seemed sincere, loving and kind, and the beautiful music, I felt good. But I still wasn't a believer. Yet. Then I heard the pastor say something profound. He said "Some of you can't or won't receive God as your heavenly father because your earthly father was either bad or absent." My heart broke. Tears began to flow freely. The pastor's words touched my soul and released me. That day, I met God.

Each Sunday, I asked Him something in secret, and every Sunday, He answered. I called every man I knew and told him not to call me anymore. The emptiness had been filled. Larry and I eventually married, had two children, and started a church. My time with him healed many wounds; however, my growth and development were not complete. I truly loved and respected Larry, but he was not perfect. He was a sincere man of God, but he was very harsh and abrasive. He used his words to both heal and wound both me and our kids. If his abuse had been physical, I would have walked away. But I believed he was the man God put in my life; I had a dilemma.

His past life was hard. On the streets of St. Louis, he got addicted to heroin. He beat the addiction, but that street-mentality became a part of him. I felt as though I was being built up and broken down at the same time. It felt strange to want to leave a man who didn't cheat or beat on me. I didn't know how to explain that I wanted to divorce the man that God gave me because he was harsh. More importantly, I found it difficult to reconcile that a loving and kind God would give me such a man. So I stayed and prayed and went to church, hoping for a change.

After 19 years of marriage, Larry had grown some, but not enough for me or our children to survive his personality. I was ready to leave my husband and disappoint God if I had to. I went to God a final time with my plans of escape. I told Him when my youngest son turned 18, I was leaving Larry and, perhaps, God's assignment for my life. I apologized to Him, because I actually wanted to finish the journey, but I simply could not. In a still, small voice, He said, "Daughter, you have no idea what tomorrow will bring."

The next year, Larry's kidneys began to fail due to a long history of diabetes and his history of drug and alcohol abuse. The sickness came quickly, hard, and painful. Our kids and I sat and watched Larry shrivel down to skin and bones. His assignment was coming to an end, and our prayers and faith couldn't stop it. I begged God not to take Larry. He simply replied, "Larry is coming home. It's your time to carry on the assignment."

I felt duped. I felt as though I had been promised better. I had thought getting the man God had for me would resulted in an easier road with a happier ending. Apparently not. Still, after Larry died on Saturday, I was in the pulpit preaching on Sunday. People marveled at my strength and my ability to keep going. My business grew exponentially, and with it came more responsibilities. Our youngest son was hit the hardest. He struggled in school and, at 17, decided not to return. Our oldest moved far away from us and dealt with his pain alone. I continued my assignment with minimal complaint, but with little joy and many tears.

Passing the Torch

I didn't pray much after Larry died. My prayer time turned into time to eat and drink more wine than I should. I gained 30 pounds in a year. I was too busy, dizzy all the time, and swamped in debt. I thought I was dying. My only request of God was, "Please don't let me die because my son can't take it." I was afraid to talk to Him more, because I wasn't ready to deal with the truths He revealed at the time of Larry's death. My plan was to serve Him from a safe distance.

When things don't make sense to me, it bothers me deeply. What in the hell was the Larry thing all about? Why grow my business at a time in which my emotional and physical strength were depleted? Why would you leave me and take Larry? Boys need their fathers during adolescence. Why take the pastor of a church and leave the pastor's wife knowing full well that our denomination doesn't support women pastors?

I struggled with my questions. Then, out of the blue, an answer emerged. "Death is more than just the cessation of life. It is a passing of the torch." When a man or woman dies, their God-given assignment gets passed from one generation to the next. When my father died, I inherited his intellect and sense of duty. This sense prompted me to pursue my education and eventually run my own business. Today, God uses this business to hire friends and family members. Larry's tough nature made me tough. The thing I hated the most about him was the thing that I would eventually need to endure – the emotional onslaught experienced by pastors while serving broken people.

I have grown to love and appreciate the person I have become. I have been shaped by the lives and deaths of three strong forces in my life. The fruit that I now bear, bears witness that my pain has and will forever be someone else's gain. Thank you Daddy. Thank you, Larry. Thank you, God!!!

This is my story, but it is not my life.

TRACY, ATLANTA, GA

My deepest fear is not that I am inadequate. My deepest fear is that death will rob me of the loved ones I cherish and hold so dear. I experienced what no child should ever have to experience. On February 24, 1971, my sweet mother died at the age of 40 and left behind a husband and seven children – three daughters from 11 months to 25 years and four sons from 4 to 16. My maternal grand-mother died the same day 10 years later. My mother was born August 15, 1930, and my mother's mom was born August 15, 1915. Mother and daughter were born on the same day and died on the same day.

I remember all too well the day my father, mother, uncle, and sister took mother to the city to go to the hospital. She was sick with a bad headache. This was something that had plagued my mom for some time, but this one was more severe and lasted longer than most. Big Mama stayed with us. My dad and sister sat in the back seat with Mama stretched across their laps. About half way to the hospital, Daddy said the weight of Mama's head seemed heavier. He looked down and saw liquid running out of the side of her mouth, and he knew Mama was passing away. He said he didn't know what to do or how to feel, but he knew he could not let my sister and uncle know what was taking place. My sister no-ticed the liquid running out of the side of Mama's mouth and commented that Mama must have been in a deep sleep. Dad did not want to frighten my sister, so he went along with her assessment.

When they arrived at the hospital, Mama was pronounced dead. There were no cell phones then, so it wasn't until Dad came back home that we knew our lives had changed forever. When Dad gave Big Mama the news, I heard sobs, then Dad went out of the back door into the field behind our house, and Big Mama came into the front room. She told us that Mama was gone. We would be coming to live with her. My older brother went to the bedroom and cried. Everyone in the house was sad, but the youngest of us did not have a clue what death was. All we knew was Mama left and never came back.

When Dad came back into the house, eyes red, and face wet from crying, we questioned him about when Mama was coming home. And he couldn't really talk about it. All I wanted was for my mommy to come home. I wanted to see my mother, a sharecropper, and self-proclaimed hair stylist, making ladies hair look beautiful. I loved to watch her work and was intrigued by how she was able to transform the overall look of women by doing their hair.

I was born into poverty. There was no running water or inside plumbing in my house until I turned 9 years old. By the world's standards, we were poor, but we were never hungry, dirty, or without clothes and shoes to wear. Most important, though, we were surrounded by love, respect, and admiration for one other. Our family values were love for family, our relationship with Jesus Christ, and serving our community. We grew most of our own food, and we shared our harvest of fruits and vegetables and our meat with our community. All seven of the children were birthed at home and delivered with the assistance of a midwife, the same one who delivered my father. For the longest time, I never knew that babies were actually born any other way.

After it sunk in that my mother was not coming home, I felt as though we had done something as children that made her leave us. I was scared, I was sad and as I got older, I felt abandoned and angry. At the funeral, I remember standing with my siblings in front of Mama's coffin like we were waiting for her to wake up. I was empty. I cried. I was angry, and I wanted my mother! We moved in with Big Mama, who was also caring for my uncle who had returned home from the war. A few years later, Big Mama's oldest son and his wife divorced. He and several of his children came to live with us, too. At 64, Big Mama was raising a second generation of babies.

The older I got, the angrier I became. By the time that I was a pre-teen, I was short-tempered and had a chip on my shoulder. Children can be cruel and even back then, whenever there was a disagreement, saying something about my mama was sure to get a rise out of me. The loss of my mother left such a gaping hole in my heart, a sense of loss of identity, and a feeling of abandon-ment. Fortunately, Big Mama, although not an educated woman, knew the word of God, and she was a praying woman. She prayed out loud every morn-ing and every night before bed, and since I shared a room with Big Mama, I heard her talk to God a lot. She talked about everything imaginable. She always started her prayers thanking God for who He was and all that He had done. She prayed for the sick, the poor, the lost, and for each of her chil-dren and grandchildren by name. Her prayers were very long, and they covered everything. I wanted to be like Big Mama when I grew up.

In high school, my behavior was negative. I was being sent home often because of fighting. If anyone said the wrong thing to me or any of my siblings, I was a force to be reckoned with. One particular morning during my eleventh grade year, the driver's education teacher took me home, because I was fighting again. When I walked in the door, Big Mama told me to get a switch. She said she knew when I left home, my spirit wasn't right and I'd be sent home.

She sat me down and told me a lot of things I needed to hear: that I had to get over being angry about losing my mother; how much she loved me; that Mama's death was not my fault; and that God was not punishing me. She explained to me that some things we would be able to understand better in the next life. She told me the huge chip on my shoulder was about me being controlled by the forces of evil; my behavior was only hurting me and making my future less bright. She affirmed me and told me I was loved, valued, and beautiful. She reminded me God had great plans for my life once I made peace with my pain of losing Mama and came to terms with my anger. Then she whipped my butt and put me on punishment. I was suspended from school for a week, something that had become standard for me.

Big Mama was our rock. She was the epitome of faith, a true woman of God, and a true servant to the community. She taught us the importance of prayer, forgiveness, servanthood, and the importance of living a sold out life for Christ Jesus. She never gave up on any of us, and I thought she could do no wrong. She never complained, never had a harsh word to say, never wavered in her faith, and never saw her task of raising children as a burden. She always wore a smile on her face and made each of us feel like we were the most important people in the world. She was definitely a saint, and I never ever wanted to lose her. She was my confidant and truest friend.

When I graduated high school and went to college I finally made peace with the demons that had taunted me for most of my young life. I give credit to Big Mama for that. When I married my high school sweetheart at the age of 20, I longed for my mother's words of wisdom and her presence as I planned a wedding and life with my husband. Big Mama was right by my side every step of the way. I longed for Mama all my life, but I have accepted there was purpose in my pain. Because of my loss at such an early age and because of my grandmother's persistence and dedication to helping me to know Jesus as Lord, I know Him as a mother to my motherless heart.

I know He loves me unconditionally. When I lost my grandmother 17 years after my mother died, I experienced the same feelings of loss and abandonment. But when Big Mama died, I understood that I was not being punished by God. After Big Mama's death, I found out about her pact with my mother. Mama asked Big Mama to raise her children if she died first, and Big Mama agreed. One of Big Mama's most fervent prayers was that God would allow her to live until we were grown. God honored her prayer. Big Mama died the month after my youngest sister graduated from high school. Her death cut like a knife, but I knew Big Mama's work on earth was done. She fought a good fight; she kept the faith and finished her course. She earned her just reward.

The children she raised have beautiful memories of her – a woman with giant faith. I thank her for teaching me to trust again, how to love, and to know that I belong to Jesus Christ. Now a mother of three and a grandmother of two, I know there is nothing more beautiful than the life that I have been given. My faith is unshakable. Truth is, the pain that I suffered as a little girl served as a catalyst to make me the woman, the wife, the mother, and the grandmother that God created me to be. Because of my experiences, I long to be a Godly mother to my children – one who loves unconditionally and seeks to lead her children and family by example. I hold them tight and show love to them every day, while giving them enough room to soar and become the people God predestined them to be. My experiences taught me the importance of living in the moment.

I know that I will see my mother and Big Mama again, but while I am blessed with the gift of life, I am compelled to live it to the fullest, putting God at the center of it all and trusting His very plan for my life, purpose, and destiny. He is working it out for my good and preparing the way for me to walk out my destiny steps on this journey called life.

This is my story, but it is not my life.

ANGELIA, BUFORD, GA

LOVE AND FORGIVENESS

I came from a Christian family that believes in marriage. Both sets of grandparents and all of my parent's siblings were married for 20 and 30 years or more. Nearly all of my male cousins have been married, but of my female cousins, only two have been married. The rest of us are single or too young to get married. Marriage didn't seem optional. It was expected. So as a single 41-year-old who has spent the last 10 years searching for peace, I am victorious in that I have found peace. I share my story with the hope that others will find peace, too, despite disappointment, rejection or heartbreak.

Studies say 43 percent of Black women will never marry. I knew it was a possibility, but I held onto hope that these dismal odds would not predict my fate. Ebony magazine printed an article that countered this data. It said 70 percent of college educated Blacks were married by the age of 40. Being part of that demographic, I held on to that glimmer of hope through my 30s. But when my fortieth and forty-first birthdays came and went, my hope that I would defy the odds dimmed.

When I was 12 years old, my mother sat me down at the kitchen table so we could talk. She looked at me with a serious expression. My mind was racing, trying to determine what I had done wrong. Then her look softened slightly and she said, "I want you to understand something. In this world, the only person that you can depend on is you." I was hurt by these words and quickly jumped in with a counter argument that made perfect sense to me. I said, "That's not true. I can always count on you and Dad." Her face did not soften one bit when she said, "There will be times when even we won't be able to help you."

I'm not sure why my mother felt the need to give me this message then. My junior high school years had been challenging. I struggled to find a place where I fit in, which left me feeling depressed and asking my mother why it seemed that no one liked me. Maybe she had grown weary of hearing me complain about how people had disappointed me. Perhaps she wanted to give me a Cliff Notes introduction to the fact that people will disappoint you many times in life. Whatever the reason or the motivation for that sudden and succinct lecture, from that day forward, I knew that the only choice I had was independence.

As I got older, many of my female friends said their mothers had similar mantras. Apparently, the world did not have fairy tales to deliver for girls. Comfort would most likely be found through our own hard work and tenacity.

I did not date growing up. I grew up in Utah in a Mormon community. My parents moved away from their hometowns in North Carolina to build careers and experience something different than the small Southern town life. My parents were the first in their families to go away to college, leave agricultural and factory life behind, and attempt to see more of the world. After my father's brief time in the military, they ended up in Utah, which wasn't necessarily a bad thing, unless you happen to be Black and Baptist like us.

I commend the Mormon Church for their support of family life. Most of my friends grew up knowing exactly how life would roll out for them. They would graduate from high school, start college or working, all the while writing to their missionary (usually a high school or college boyfriend who was away serving a required two-year mission for The Church). When their missionary returned, they would marry, hopefully finish their education, and have kids. It was a nearly fail-proof plan. Dating, for them, was very serious business. In high school, good Mormon girls and boys did not date for fun, but for marriage. I, on the other hand, went through my entire high school career without being asked on one date, primarily because I was not Mormon and did not fit into this well-laid plan. It is a very unique experience to grow up in a world where dating and marriage is expected of everyone except you.

I went to one of the larger Black Baptist churches in the state, and thankfully I was able to recruit a date or two from this pool of respectable young black men. But I had to ask them out, and their mothers would not allow them to say no. Thanks to this band of outsiders, I was able to attend a total of four dances during high school.

I learned to focus on my grades and extracurricular activities. In hindsight, I'm thankful for that experience because it taught me my value beyond the context of romantic relationships. I was a straight-A student and a competitive member of the science, math, and debate club. I studied ballet, performed in theatre, and even won a spot at the prestigious Governor's Honors Academy summer program. When I graduated from high school, I attended an historically black college in the South. My experience there was a much different one. I got plenty of attention from the opposite sex. One of my classmates didn't understand why I hadn't dated in high school because, she said, I would have been the Black man's dream in Brooklyn, where she grew up. My inexperience in high school made this attention a little overwhelming. It was nice to know that I was seen as attractive, but it seemed that the focus was more on sex, rather than love and commitment. Not knowing how to navigate, I stumbled my way through one bad relationship after another. I would either fall in love with a guy whose intention was never to love me back or be so jaded from those experiences that I overlooked or mistreated guys who were looking for true love. This pattern continued through graduate school and even into the early part of my career. While it was disheartening, I was young and resilient and still maintained hope I would find "the one."

My mother's pep-talk about independence served me well. I was really okay if I didn't get married until I was established in my career. In my mind, things would work themselves out, and I would be happily married by the age of 29. This was the deadline. But my birthday came and went with no marriage and during that year, a couple of life events happened that changed my perspective and sense of urgency. My father passed away, and I was laid off from my job. The two things that had always been consistent in my life; my parents and my ability to excel through academia or career, were slipping away, and I had no one to lean on. I wanted someone who could be there for me, hold my hand, and tell me things would be okay, that I would be okay. In our youth, our parents serve this role. But as an adult, your partner should be able to fill that void. The family of my youth was disappearing, and I did not yet have my own family. I realized the number of people in this world that would love me unconditionally was finite and getting smaller.

Without a job, I was also left to try and define myself without a professional role. I could always look to achievements (academic, professional, cultural) to validate my worth, my contribution to the world, my purpose. During my 30s, my career was back on track, and I progressed financially. I bought my first home on my own, became better at selecting more genuine men and got out of bad and one-sided relationships quickly.

In my 40s, I have accepted the idea that marriage is maybe not a definite. I've forgiven my exes and myself for the past heart breaks. I have had the luxury of time to define life and success on my own terms, to spend time in prayer and meditation, and learn a dependence on God that I'm not sure would have been the same had I been a wife or a mother. I became comfortable and pray my heart will remain open. My life is easy; it's peaceful and stable. Even if faced with challenges, I know God will work them out for my good. He always has. I have decided that married or not, I want the experience of motherhood and am moving forward to make that a reality, with God guiding my path. I still have a tiny mustard seed of faith that marriage will be part of my story. I planted that seed in my heart and protect it. I feed it daily with prayer, and I peacefully stand in the truth that, even if it never happens, I will have joy. I will live life to the fullest. I will give and receive love. I will let my light shine. And I will not apologize for how brightly I shine.

This is my story, but it is not my life.

ANGELA, BOISE, ID

I remember the first time I fell in love. The kind of love that makes you lose your mind and sacrifice your principles, self-worth, and common sense. The desperate kind of love that makes you forget your good upbringing. Yeah, that love. The pattern for what I thought was a relationship was set for many years to come, 15 years to be exact.

On October 24, 1979, I went with a cousin to a bar she heard was fairly decent. The bartender called out to introduce me to his brother, who was sitting at the bar. The bartender's brother had been nursing a drink, not paying attention to anything around him. When he turned around and smiled, I melted. Of course I joined him at the bar when he asked.

We talked for hours until the bar closed. He was intelligent, a great conversationalist, and a good listener. We talked about parents, upbringing, school, work, and relationships. He was exactly my age, 9 days older than me, and perfect in every way, except there was just this one, tiny issue…he was married, but separated. After hearing his tragic story, I was drawn into him, wanting to nurture and save him from his misery. Somehow in my mind, I considered the marriage to be over and convinced myself I was dating a single man.

He had moved back to his parents' home after his wife left him. I met his friends and his entire family. His sister and I became great friends for many years. Even in later years, long after we broke up and I moved to another state, his father still told him, "Son, you should have married that girl." I was happier than I had ever been in my life.

As the relationship progressed, he consistently behaved badly, which I excused, accepted and absorbed, just to make him happy. By the end of our 3rd year together, something changed. He started drifting away. I didn't know what to think, but knew something was terribly wrong. Eventually, I discovered he had a new girlfriend and had filed to divorce his wife.

I don't remember the details of our break up. I just know it happened in early May, 1984. I was fully awake early one morning when my mind somehow drifted into unfamiliar territory, almost as if I was in a dream state, but I wasn't dreaming. My thinking and demeanor were clear, calm, and matter-of-fact like. I wasn't angry at all. I just remember thinking, "I want to hurt him." I was dead serious. It was as rational to me as if I had said, "I have to go to the bathroom." My mind then drifted further down a dark and dangerous path--- I couldn't stop it. I didn't want to stop it. It didn't make sense to stop it. Earlier than usual the next morning, the phone suddenly rang. An older gentleman who befriended me months earlier, who didn't know me well enough to call me at that hour of the morning, was on the other line. He immediately became alarmed and pressed me to tell him what was wrong. At some point, I came to myself and broke down in tears. The full seriousness of what I was thinking came to me, and I realized how dangerously close I had gotten to the edge of sanity. Later, I asked my friend what made him call that morning. He told me he had a nagging feeling that just wouldn't go away, and against his better judgment, called me anyway.

Even though I had not been in church for many years, I knew the hand of God when I saw it. What I do know for certain is, if God hadn't intervened, this "love" could have nearly cost me my sanity, freedom, and perhaps even my life.

While I never again dated another married man, there were times over the next 10 years that I knowingly allowed myself to be the other woman; the side-chick. Some of the more memorable men are: the guy I grew up with who had given me a key to his house, stood me up New Years' Eve, only for me to find him in bed with another woman after a night of worrying. Then there was the guy who pretended to be gay to avoid taking me out. One boyfriend left me for a former girlfriend. There was the co-worker/lover who moved his girlfriend into the same apartment complex I lived in, while I continued to sneak around with him. There was the multi-millionaire who only wanted me for home-cooked meals and sex. There was the man I met through friends, and after a year of dating, disappeared on Valentine's Day, after sending me the most beautiful roses and card. These "relationships" always left me feeling hurt, broken, and empty. My heart felt like a wound that was constantly picked at and couldn't heal.

In January 1995, something interesting happened. I went to see an old college friend for the weekend. Except for Friday night, we spent the entire weekend in church, and I was not pleased! On Monday, my flight was suddenly cancelled! My friend said, "Good! You can go to church with me this evening!" I was *pissed*! "*More church? This chick is nuts!*" I thought to myself. That evening, the sermon spoke to my heart, and I was convicted! I understood I had allowed myself, God's child, to be mistreated all of those years. Finally, I understood the power I possessed to control exactly how I would allow someone to treat me; that my actions and what I *allowed* others to do to me actually *taught* them how to treat me. I had to have faith I could walk away from someone…*anyone*, in fact, rather than allow myself to be treated poorly. That evening, I turned my life over to God.

I joined a wonderful church back home and became an active, faithful member. Practicing my new-found power left me feeling liberated in a way I had never before felt. On October 1, a choir member told me a friend of hers wanted to meet me. I agreed and met Pierre immediately after service. Pierre was a very nice-looking man with a genuine and peaceful demeanor. That evening, we talked on the phone for hours. For once, I was not thinking about a relationship. I enjoyed the easy conversations we had over the next two weeks.

One day, something came over me. I uttered the words, *"God, thank you for my husband."* All of a sudden, a smile I did not control crept across my face, and I felt butterflies in my stomach. I heard the loud whisper-shout of God's voice to my ear saying, "He's on his way. It's soon, very soon." I started pressing God for details. "How soon is soon? I'm not even talking to anyone, well, except that Pierre guy and it's probably not him. It has to be someone I haven't met yet! Maybe we'll meet early next year!" Excitedly, I settled myself and decided to trust God and His timing. I put the thought out of my mind and decided to wait on God.

Over the next two weeks, Pierre and I went on 4 dates. He was a great guy who actually listened to me. He always honored his word and did what he said he was going to do, when he said he was going to do it. We had a lot in common, with strikingly similar upbringings. On our fourth date, Pierre told me he loved me, and that he wanted to marry me. I sort of played it off because I had put my conversation with God out of my head. A few days later, Pierre said he was serious about marriage, and he wanted us to go shopping for a ring. That's when it hit me! God's words came back to my mind, and I realized this was the man God sent me. I also realized what true love felt like. For me, it's not that desperate, heart-palpating-can't-wait-to-see-you feeling. It's the easy comfort of feeling like you just met the other half of yourself. I knew I could be the me that I was, and not try so hard to be the perfect person; that I was already fearfully and wonderfully made – in His image and likeness. I understood what "soul mate" felt like. When I asked Pierre what made him want to meet me, he told me I wasn't the person he wanted to meet. The person who introduced us got me mixed up with another church member! So 4 ½ weeks after meeting, we became engaged, and 3 months later, on February 10, 1996, we married. We've now been happily married for 20 years, and remain active members of our church, giving God the praise and glory for His greatness in our lives.

This is my story, but it is not my life.

DENISE, CHICAGO, IL

"Even Jesus makes you ask for forgiveness," I haughtily said in a discussion with some co-workers, when we were discussing forgiving those who had personally wronged us or our families. I was remembering how some people had, years before, hurt my family, after my parents had done so much to help them. "Why should I forgive someone who isn't sorry for what they have done?" I asked, quite sure in my rightness and refusing to even listen to another side on the issue.

My parents had helped so many people through the years, though they had little money themselves. We often had people stay with us through my childhood, people who were going through rough patches, whether they had hit hard times as they struggled with divorce, war trauma, family strife, or other life events or whether they were climbing their way back up in their battles with alcoholism, drug addiction, or other issues. My parents never complained. They believed they were supposed to help their family and friends however they could. Some thanked them and appreciated the help; some never did. A small few seemed to turn on them, taking advantage of the love and support and hurt them in the process. My parents did not deserve that, and after multiple affronts, my protective instincts kicked in, and when opportunity presented itself, my vicious tongue struck like a snake, lashing out at them. I banished a couple of those persons from the circle of my family and friends so they could not hurt my parents or any of my family members again.

When someone hurts anyone I love, my anger can resemble that of a Momma Bear. I rarely feel sorry for the damage I inflict when I feel my anger is justified, and I really do not care about the consequences I may face.

Years later, the anger still boiled up inside me as I remembered the hurt and disappointment my parents and the rest of the family felt when my cousin stole from us to support his drug habit. Why should I forgive that act when he hadn't even apologized? How could someone suggest I do that when they weren't there? They didn't see the hurt on my mother's face, the disappointment in my father's eyes, or hear the pain in my uncles' voices. He'd stolen from his family and made excuses.

I discussed it with my husband, who patiently and steadfastly listened to my rants. I hadn't even heard from this cousin. Why was this eating on me if everyone I cared about agreed that I was right?

Then, the voice whispered to me. I pictured God sending his guardian angels to whisper in my ear and the angels wearily shaking their head, "Here she goes again…" as they contemplated whether to bang on drums to get my attention or just wait until I exhausted myself. But I heard Him ask, "How can someone apologize to you if you don't know where he is? If you don't know where he is, do you think he can find you? Do I make it this hard for you to be forgiven?"

My haughtiness halted. I was momentarily humbled, as I tried to find a way around these questions in my head. I thought I was a good person, and a fair person, and suddenly, I didn't feel so right or fair anymore. I decided that to relieve my own conscience, I should try to find him and give him the chance to apologize. Dang it. I didn't like feeling wrong. I set out to find him, secretly hoping I wouldn't find him so I could still be right. After all, it had been close to 20 years, and he had lived on the periphery of society. Surely, there would be no way I would find him! Right? Of course, not. I found him within a day. God was determined I would find him.

He was living in the back of someone's car repair shop, sleeping on a cot, several states away. He had sunk so low in life that he had barely more than the clothes on his back, and was living in the back of the shop where he worked. He had been punished for hurting my family, and with no one to hold up a higher standard of hope for him, he had fallen mighty low. He was ecstatic to hear from me, and as God knew he would, he immediately apologized for everything he had done to my parents, the rest of my family, and to me. He had damaged his own life more than he had ever damaged any of ours. He had no hard feelings at all toward me. He told me he loved me still, and how much he had missed the rest of our family and me. I was humbled, and I cried. My heart practically burst with the joy of forgiveness, and the love I had suppressed. Why had I held onto this anger so long, and for what purpose? I read in an old Cherokee tale once, "When you feed hate and do not forgive, it is like drinking poison and expecting the other person to die." The Bible is full of verses on the importance of forgiving others as you want God to forgive you, so why did I not forgive more freely?

My cousin has moved closer to me, and he has re-built his life from ashes. He has a steady job, a house, and is getting married in a few months. We have helped him along the way, and he cannot do enough to thank me and repay me. There are still those in the family who do not treat him well, but that is between God and them. I cannot cure any hearts but my own. I know how hard it is to forgive, but I have learned the importance of it, for oneself and one's peace, if not for others. I know that, for me, the cost of bitterness in my soul was not worth whatever benefit I thought I was getting, and love and forgiveness shine much more beautifully in my soul than the ugliness of grudges and hate.

I spoke to an old friend recently whom I was helping with a legal matter. This man had served time in prison for something he did over 15 years ago, and many still judged him for it, even though he has long since served his time. While in prison, he studied the Bible, and became so fascinated with the story of Job that he began to shave his own head everyday as a reminder of repentance and humility. After his release from prison, he has done many truly good and selfless acts that have cost him, financially and otherwise, for no other reason than he believed it was the right thing to do. One thing in particular moved me so deeply that, in spite of my own progress with forgiveness, I realized I still have much to learn. My friend was told when he was released from prison, he was to stay away from the victim's family. He, however, read the Bible and knew the importance of forgiveness. He said, "I could not have that man's hate on me because I know that anyone with hate in their heart is separated from God, and I needed to know that I had done everything I could do to help that man be at peace with me." So, upon being released from prison, he went straight to the victim's house to sincerely and deeply apologize. The man forgave him, and they shared a meal together. The state penal system was not so forgiving, and my friend was thrown back in jail for several months for violating parole. He told me he knew that was going to be the outcome of his visit, but the other man's peace and forgiveness were that important to him. He went to jail so the other man would not be filled with hate; so the man would not be separated from God. I was incredibly humbled. Would I have gone so far to have been forgiven? How many people would?

I cannot say that giving forgiveness comes easy. I do not know why I sometimes hang onto things that cause me pain when I know I shouldn't. My stubborn pride and protective instinct still kick in when someone I love is hurt. The Momma Bear in me still wants to keep them safe, to strike back hard and fast at anyone who dares to hurt someone I love and cherish. The temptation to mentally punish someone who deserves it is real for me, but I know it is damaging to me more than them and not worth the sacrifice. I need forgiveness from those whom I have hurt, and I need to give it more freely and quickly to those who have hurt my loved ones or me. I thank God He does not make it so hard to be forgiven, and I thank him for sending angels like my friend who went to prison in order to be forgiven. My friend has shown me the importance of forgiveness, whether someone asks for it or not.

His story makes me want to strive to be better person. I now understand that withholding forgiveness blots my own soul, not anyone else's, and what an amazing gift forgiveness is in that it can bring the giver even more blessings and beauty than it does the receiver.

This is my story, but it is not my life.

KAYE, HOMER, LA

"...we are members of one another"
—*Ephesians* 4:25

About Awesome Life Ministries

Live Your Awesome Life Ministries is an off-shoot of my blog of three years LIVE YOUR AWESOME LIFE ONE OOPS AT A TIME (www.liveyourawesomelife.com).

When the blog reached nearly 200,000 readers, God instructed me to create a ministry for women.

My goal is for the ministry to be a transparent, real, inviting and safe place for all women who are in Christ or looking for Christ in their lives. A place to share our truth.

About the Author

I grew up in Salt Lake City, Utah to a single parent. I was the first to attend college. I attended both Howard University and Harvard Business School. I have built my career as a marketing consultant in communications. I have been married for 24 years and have two beautiful children.

I am active in church in Atlanta, have traveled to over 35 countries and enjoy community service.

I have a passion for teaching, speaking and facilitating, especially to young people and women.

My goal in life is to be a great ambassador to the world of God's goodness in my life. We serve an awesome God.

I hope this will become my first of many books to come.